SURVIVAL OF THE DANGLY GREEN PARROT EARRINGS

by BONNIE L. BAIRD

SURVIVAL OF THE DANGLY GREEN PARROT EARRINGS

Copyright © 2016 Bonnie Baird

Published by Bonnie Baird

Cover Art Design © Croco Designs

Edited by The Red Pen Coach

All rights reserved.

This book is for your personal enjoyment only. It may not be resold, given away, copied, transmitted, stored in a retrieval system or reproduced in any manner whatsoever without written permission of the author, except in the case of brief quotations contained in articles and reviews.

I have tried to recreate events, locales and conversations from my memories of them. In order to maintain their anonymity in some instances I have changed the names of individuals and places, I may have changed some identifying characteristics and details such as physical properties, occupations and places of residence.

ISBN 978-0-9940973-3-0 (print book)

ISBN 978-0-9940973-0-9 (electronic book)

Select titles also by Bonnie L. Baird

Poetry

I Smell Stars:
Final Twelve Years of a Marriage

Walk Me to the Door, Love:
Notes Written to the Beloved in the First Two Years of Grief

Lightening Strikes:
Complicated Family Relationships

Close to the Undertow:
On the Practice of Ministry

CD

I Smell Stars

Walk Me to the Door, Love

Acknowledgements

Thank you to all my readers who waded through ponderous versions of this book, especially to Bishop Sue Moxley, Bonnie Hebb and Borden Conrad. Your suggestions and feedback kept me on track. Love the title you suggested Borden!

This book would have remained in a desk drawer without the inspiration and mentorship of my friend Heather D. Veinotte. Thank you, Heather, for your patience and unflagging support. I always enjoy our writing times carved out of busy days. And reading your books.

And then there are the editors, Donna Alward whose gentle persistence produced a much tighter and more honest work, and Nancy Cassidy of The Red Pen Coach editing company who agreed to take on this project. Bless both of you! Frauke Spanuth of Croco Designs produced a parrot earring I wish I owned: thank you for your design and formatting skills.

Lines of poetry quoted in this book are from my book *Close to the Undertow*, poetic reflections on the experience of ministry.

This book is dedicated to Dave,
fellow traveller through ministry.
Thank you for the journey and the company.

Table of Contents

To Begin With…	15
Around the Altar	17
• First Time, Just Before Ordination	17
• Best Amen	18
• Bearing the Chalice	19
• Youth Group	20
• Memory: Seeking the Light	22
Liminal Space	23
Bullies by Any Other Name	27
• Colleagues	27
• They Hunt in Packs	29
When Death Comes Calling	35
• Not Invited	35
• When the Band Played	37
• Who's to Blame?	39
It Happened in the Hospital	43
• Bodily Functions and an Inexperienced Priest	43
• Absolution	44
• Buns of Steel and Homemade Bread	46
• Even the Sparrow	50
• Oh, Crap!	52
• The Nature of Shame	54
The Sacredness of Buildings	57
• Rearranging the Furniture	58
• Room to Swing a Casket	59
• Not in Vain	62
• Last Service	65
• Taking Down a Church	68
• Reclamation	72
Let's Start a Rumour	77
The Minister Doesn't Visit	81
Preaching Without Notes	83
Always Check the Readings of the Day	87
The Vows We Make	91

BUT WILL THE GOWN STILL FIT?	
AND SOME BAPTISMS TO REMEMBER	**99**
• George	103
• Sunrise Service	104
• Grandson	105
IT'S NOT JUST FUNDRAISING	**109**
• The Launch	109
• Flowers for Cancer	112
• ATV Run	114
• Define Success	117
• Lighting the Night	119
GOD IN THE BUDGET	**123**
ENTERTAINING ANGELS UNAWARE	**127**
• Memory: A Student's Perspective	127
• Feeding the Hungry	129
• Against All Odds	132
• Anyone For a Lift?	134
• No New Members	138
• Across Old Divides	139
THE LINES WE CROSS	**145**
YOU CAN NEVER GO BACK	**151**
SO YOU WANT TO BE A MINISTER…	**157**

To Begin With...

The ministry...oh, such work to give one's heart to. Sometimes, over the years, I wished I could have turned back the clock and gone back to a regular job.

There would have been no working late into the evenings, or that sense of being on call for anything, or getting up in the middle of the night for the long drive to the hospital and the lonely walk down an echoing corridor to a too-still room. I signed up for navigating the waves of the human soul—the heights and depths of life with little calm sailing.

I am, in some ways, displaced right now. I have plunged into full-time ministry again after a brief retirement. Unlike most who inhabit this village in which I live and work, I have no deep roots here.

Only one place has ever been home to me: the get-away-from-work retreat which became our retirement home, situated on the shores of a large lake in the interior of Nova Scotia. The name *The Lakehouse*, which I preferred, never caught on for some reason. My husband Dave, our son, and now our grandsons, have only ever known it as *The Cottage*.

Dave and I spent many years there, trekking to it from our day jobs on Friday nights, looking forward to the isolation and the wildness of the place. We would place a log in the woodstove and break out the wine and books.

We treasured our times there, sitting in the starry night,

our conversations weaving together as we wrapped up the day. We enjoyed walking down country roads, our dog sniffing somewhere in the undergrowth.

All that is gone now. My husband died a few years ago, and I am now rector of another parish.

I was ordained in 1994 as a deacon in the Anglican Church of Canada. About six months later, I became a priest.

"But, Mom," my little son said to me at the time, "my teacher says only Roman Catholics can become priests."

Not so, or I would certainly have been excluded. In the Anglican Church of Canada, men *and* women are ordained as deacons, priests, bishops.

I have worked as an ordained clergy (deacon, priest, minister, pastor, vicar) in New Brunswick along the Fundy Shore, in Nova Scotia along the South Shore, as well as on the edge of Halifax. I have been a student, a rector with the responsibility of overseeing a parish in four different places, and an interim clergy filling in between rectors in two parishes. I acted briefly as one of the bishop's archdeacons—a pastoral troubleshooter on the ground.

In that time, I have witnessed much that is beautiful and much that is awful, and sometimes I have seen both wrapped so tightly together you couldn't tear them apart. If my younger self met me now, she would encounter a stranger.

There are so many memories. Most reveal the brokenness and beauty of people reaching for something, or Someone, beyond themselves. These are the liminal moments of people's lives in which a clergy stands; sacred spaces that can leave you shaken, speechless, inadequate to the task, and blessed. And there's a thin line between not getting too close, or being too distant, which all clergy walk with various degrees of success.

These memories tuck around me like a patchwork quilt drawn up to the chin.

Share a bit of time with me? Let me bend your ear.

Around the Altar

First Time, Just Before Ordination

I had never been part of an altar guild, and had never helped clean a church. I had always been at a safe distance, in a choir stall or in the congregation, except of course when I was a student setting the table in school, or in a field placement. The quiet day, or Day of Second Thoughts, ended with me behind the white pine altar, the large-print book of instructions, prayers, and services (missal) to my left, and the church empty except for my priest. Tomorrow I would be priested. There was still so much to learn.

Remnants of what various clergy had said floated by me:

"This is sacred ground, the holiest place in the church." *I suppose he meant the building and not the people.*

"Only the priest is allowed behind the altar." *I'm not supposed to be here.*

"Always acknowledge the altar when crossing in front of it." *Wasn't all that head bobbing a distraction to the people?*

"Now begin the prayer," my priest said from the back of the church.

That's it?

Having watched countless clergy celebrate the Eucharist, I knew the right motions to make and when to make them, though I was uncomfortable with the frequent crosses some priests made over the bread and the wine. Unlike a number of my colleagues, I would never kiss the altar; I imagined altar guilds upset with lipstick marks on the fair linen. I liked the minimalist way my priest celebrated, with each action easily understood by the people.

I began the prayer. A stillness settled upon me and my focus narrowed. My arms seemed to rise on their own as I repeated the words of institution: "Take, eat, this is my body given for you…Drink this all of you…my blood shed for you." I held the bread and wine up to God and out to an imaginary people. Time elongated. Only the words mattered. In the beginning was the Word expressing the inexpressible; there was only the people, and the One in whose name I was speaking and remembering.

Years later, a visiting bishop from the States commented, "The older I get, the more I realize my role is to simply get out of the way of the Spirit."

No bread or wine was blessed that afternoon in the quiet of the church. It wouldn't have been holy in any case. Yet something else was blessed. Something deep inside whispered, *It's okay to be you.*

Best Amen

Holy Eucharist, Holy Communion, the Lord's Supper, the Great Thanksgiving—the sacrament has many names. The one I favour, I encountered many years ago at the altar rail. I use the others more frequently, but the name that my heart responds to in its deepest recesses is the Great Thanksgiving.

I had known the child since before he was born. His mom and dad were newly married and excited at the prospect of being parents. They wanted to do everything by the book, including making sure their child would grow up in the church. During my first visit to them, I was shown the printout of the ultrasound. I couldn't distinguish one end from the other, but they kept pointing out features. We discussed the awesome responsibility ahead of them, and wondered together what the child she was carrying would be like.

Their son was born in the spring. He was baptized soon afterward in the midst of a community that eagerly proclaimed their care of this child of God, and of his parents who had grown up in the village. "Will you who witness these vows, do all in your power to support these persons in their life in Christ?" I asked.

"We will," they responded as one.

Under the watchful eyes of his church family, he grew from babe-in-arms to exploring toddler—watch those candles, servers, in case they get bumped—to little boy. We marvelled at his first words, first steps, first being able to sit still for more than five minutes. We watched him standing mid-aisle, dancing to the guitars and drums, tried not to smile as he swung from the altar rail or hung onto his mom when she went up to read a Scripture lesson, or pounded one end of the keyboard his dad was trying to play.

Now, at three, he was learning the proper way to receive the holy bread during Eucharist. He walked up the aisle beside his mom and knelt down beside her that Sunday, mimicking each movement she made. He held up his little hands, right over left, in a cup shape. I carefully placed a piece of the bread in his palms. "The body of Christ given for you," I said.

"What do you say?" his mom prompted in a stage whisper, nudging him gently with her elbow. He looked down at the bread in his hands for a long moment, then up at me.

He grinned and said in a voice that rang through the church, "Thanks!"

Bearing the Chalice

There are many perils implicit in being a chalice bearer (the person who offers or administers the wine to others during

Communion). For some, it is low-cut dresses. For me, it is big noses. Or pouffy hair. Or someone so tall I have to reach up to offer the cup. You can watch for telltale facial signs that the wine has reached its destination, but sometimes there are none.

I am shorter than the average person, so my preferred method of approach is to offer tall people the cup, keeping a good grip on it until it is securely passed. Dropping a full chalice is not a pretty spectacle. Some people refuse to take hold of it for whatever reason.

He was a tall, slender, well-groomed man in his mid-forties. His waxed handlebar moustache swept out past either side of his face, totally obscuring any view of his mouth.

I offered him the chalice. He didn't respond.

I positioned the half-full cup as best I could—no help there either—then began tipping it. No reaction. I tipped further. No reaction. Perhaps he was used to a more experienced chalice bearer who could better judge the level of wine in the cup.

Wine was running down his chin, over his white shirt, hitting the rail by the time I noticed. My first thought was: *That's blessed wine. We'll have to burn him now.*

Instead, I did the prudent thing. I started mopping up with the small white purificator (napkin) I used to wipe the cup. I mopped up the rail, his shirt, his moustache. "Sorry," I kept saying, over and over, as I dabbed away.

To anyone wanting to administer the wine during Communion, I will explain the hazards and the joys, and what an important and sacred ministry it is. I do not administer myself except when pressured to do so.

Youth Group

The church wanted a youth group. Parents wanted it. Church leaders wanted it. There needed to be something to keep the kids' interest in church beyond Sunday School.

Most of us had a memory of belonging to such a group. Mine was of Bible studies held in a parent's living room way out in the country. We would sit on the carpet in a semi-circle, listening to our minister, looking beyond him through large picture windows into the starry, sometimes full-mooned, night. It was a place we could share our insights without fear, where we didn't have to be quiet like in church. The evenings ended with grilled cheese sandwiches or pizza in the adjoining open kitchen. Older kids mixed with the younger ones, who were usually siblings. Parents arrived to pick us up and stopped in for a cup of coffee and some catching-up.

Who wouldn't want to recreate that?

But our demographics were wrong. We had mostly younger children in the church, and no one wanted to work with them. With older teens perhaps, but not with them.

So we tried a different approach. Eight signed up, and soon the number had grown to twenty-two. There were no minimum age limits on those who wanted to be a server during the service. They only had to be big enough to safely carry the large pavement candles down the two steps from the sanctuary into the centre of the church. One server carried the cross, two bore the candles in procession, and one handed the wine and bread to the priest as the altar was set for Communion. Older servers helped the younger ones.

On any given Sunday, if you looked across the sanctuary or up from the congregation, you would see white-gowned servers in various poses: some slumped groggily in their chairs, some trying to catch the attention of another server, some fidgeting with books or bulletins, a few alert. Most were a beat or more behind the congregation when it came to standing, sitting, or kneeling.

I thought a pep talk about following along in the prayer

books and crisply kneeling at certain points like everyone else might do the trick.

The next Sunday, I looked up to see if my instructions had been followed. All servers were kneeling at the right times; all focused on their prayer books. One was lying prone on the carpet propped up on his elbows with his book laid out before him, as relaxed as if he was reading a good book at home.

Get a life, I told my critical self.

Memory: Seeking the Light

It is Christmas Eve.

The frenzy of party going, baking, picking out gifts and wrapping them, and getting some in the mail, is over. The finger-numbing, fight-provoking decorating and tree trimming is done. Or as much done as it will be this year. It's time to put away the excesses, to shelve, for a few minutes, the worries about bills, alcoholic family members, children far away.

The midnight service is beginning.

The church is packed despite the hour.

We sit in darkness, except for the Advent wreath and its white Christmas candle in the centre. We light the first taper from the centre candle, and then light tapers from tapers, passing along the flame to each other until the inside of this place is as lit as a starry night sky.

An eight-year-old server stands in the sanctuary just inside the altar rail. His prayer book lies open on the rail. He holds his candle out over it, trying to find the words in the darkness. Light pools around him.

This is the stuff of Christmas cards. The essence of faith.

Liminal Space

It was five minutes before service and I was in the tiny vestry, gowning in preparation for worship. Mark stood in the doorway, shifting from foot to foot.

Mark was a trim, white-haired man in his seventies, with a gentle face and nature. He was a member of our 9 a.m. choir, and noticeably uncomfortable at this moment.

"Excuse me for bothering you," he said, clearing his throat. "But I wanted you to know. I got my results back this week."

He had my attention now.

"I'm terminal."

He ducked under the low doorframe and made his way back to the choir stalls. He sat down among his friends, most of them new since he'd moved into these parts a few years ago. They were new friends but good friends—all of them shared a deep love of music.

Once every month or so, they gathered at someone's home and had a kitchen party. Mark would be on fiddle or guitar, others on spoons, keyboard, drum, violin, mouth organ, or accordion. Their favourite place to play was on the deck of a friend's two-storey house, set like a ship hovering above a long narrow inlet of the sea.

One summer evening, their music drew quite a crowd. Boats stopped offshore in the bay and motors stilled as people leaned over the sides, listening.

I was invited once, though I'm not musical. I drank in the music rising around me, relaxed in a way I seldom could around others. What a gift they had. What a gift to share.

The last five minutes before service is the time most clergy are trying to focus, clear their minds, centre. Five minutes before service and here he was, bearing the news of his impending demise.

His best friend was diagnosed with terminal cancer two weeks later.

* * *

How they became friends is still a mystery to me. I couldn't imagine two men who were more different from each other.

Mark was easy-going, laughed a lot, and could pick up any musical instrument and birth a song. He preferred contemporary worship in the Book of Alternative Services (though how contemporary is a thirty-year-old prayer book?), and guitar music to that of the organ. He was open to change—hardly surprising in a songwriter. He had taught countless people how to play over the years, even some of the older members of the choir.

On my first visit to his tiny home, a few streets down from the church, I noticed a photo of musicians that looked oddly familiar. He had once belonged to a band that had travelled the length and breadth of the Ottawa Valley when I'd lived there as a teen. Their music had often played on a local radio station. I remembered the band well.

His friend, Colin, was tall and thin and in his seventies, too, and had a military background. Years before he arrived at the church, he had been in charge of a ship. He liked things orderly, scheduled. He preferred the more traditional worship in the Book of Common Prayer. He liked the cadence of the Elizabethan words he had spoken since childhood. He and I had already had one discussion on the proper response to the Gospel reading. He still said, "And with thy spirit," when everyone else responded, "And also with you."

I met him late one Saturday night when my phone rang. "I'm not connected to a church," the voice on the other end of the line said, "but I need the services of an Anglican clergy."

We sat beside his dying wife in their well-appointed, spacious home. Over cups of Earl Grey he explained how she had been sick a long, long time. He hoped he had done his best by her. "Can you say a prayer for her and for me?" he asked. The week after her funeral, he came to check out the church and stayed.

Who knows why Mark and Colin fit together so well as friends? Perhaps it was the women. Each had recently given his heart to a musical woman in the choir. Mark sang beside his love each week in church. Colin looked on admiringly from the congregation, and acted as host or audience to the kitchen parties.

* * *

The news hit the choir hard. It was bad enough one was sick, but both? They couldn't get their minds around it. When they did a heaviness settled upon them. It was hard looking into their faces at worship.

Quietly they developed a schedule (how Colin must have loved that) to sit beside the two men. Few others in the church knew about it. Each of the handful of choir members took turns. As the disease Mark and Colin shared progressed, some friends sat through the nights, too.

The week before he died, Colin managed to make it into Mark's hospital room. They'd had a good visit, the choir told me later; they worked out some details for the future. They asked to be interred in the cremation plot just outside the back door of the little church they had both loved and served.

Mark and Colin died within days of each other. Their families wanted one service for both. It would be difficult to put together the perfect interment service, I thought. How do you mix such different preferences?

On a drizzly afternoon, we gathered around the rectangular cremation plot: church and family, choir and loves. How many people had we buried there over the years?

Two deep holes, kitty-corner to each other, had been carefully dug. Two urns rested side by side. Familiar words from Scripture filled the spaces between us—some modern, some Elizabethan.

There was a certain cadence to it.

Bullies by Any Other Name

I came home crying, and Mom asked what on Earth was wrong. I told her about Margaret at school (grade three like me) who would stand behind me in class lineups and pinch me when the teacher wasn't looking.

"Next time she pinches you, wait until the teacher isn't looking and you slug her—hard," Mom said.

Dad was horrified. "You can't tell her to do that! It's not what we do in this family," he said.

"Just do it," Mom said.

The church is more like my dad than my mom, I think. It advises turning the other cheek, even the kind that is pinched and which you might want to sit on later. Isn't that what Jesus taught? Sometimes the church forgets that Jesus was no meek-mannered victim. It forgets how he stood up to evil wherever it raised its seductive or ugly head. It glosses over the cleansing of the temple and his anger.

Maybe that's why there are so many bullies in the church. I've heard many tales from friends and colleagues over the years. I have been in the thick of them too, too many times. And sometimes I have even been one.

Colleagues

It had been a difficult move away from a parish I had loved

and served many years. I was beginning to understand that things were very different here: canon (church) law, presiding with my back to the congregation (at least in my parish), and ways of relating to other clergy. It probably didn't help that I was more liberal than most, and female in a predominantly male college of clergy.

The archdeacon was the clergy responsible for overseeing my interim appointment in a new province and a new diocese. He issued the invitation to come join the other Anglican clergy in the city closest to where I was serving. "It'll be a good way for you to get to know them," he told me. I heard, *Come be colleagues with us.*

I didn't notice his startled expression when I walked into the massive stone church. *How wonderful to be with clergy again, all of us receiving Communion together*, I thought, as I made my way slowly down from the rail.

By then, I had spent too many months moving from church to church trying to find community again. Being a come-from-away was no fun at all when the rector discovered you were clergy. There were few heartfelt welcomes or invitations to lead the odd Bible study or midweek Communion. Just a curt acknowledgement: "We'll have to discuss boundaries if you want to help out."

When the position came up to take care of a parish until they hired their new rector, I took it. It involved being on the highway during the worst part of the winter, on a two-hour commute one-way several times a week. But I felt better. I was finally doing what I was called to do again.

After service, we gathered around a long table in the boardroom downstairs. A coffee urn was set up at one end. Mugs clinked and coffee flowed as the business portion of the meeting got underway. I didn't ask about the programs I hadn't heard of before; I didn't want to bring attention to an inadequacy on my part.

It was a little question, really, that I asked at the end of the meeting after everything else had been discussed. It was something to do with the imposition of ashes and where to put that into the Ash Wednesday service in the Book of Common Prayer. The date was drawing near and I wanted to be prepared, as it was the only book they used in my temporary parish. I was more familiar with the contemporary prayer book where such things were laid out. Surely, this was the place to ask the question, I thought. So many—at least a dozen—of long-time clergy were here.

My supervisor's face contorted, and his eyes narrowed as he leaned forcefully across the table and into my space. *My God, tell me what I said?* I thought frantically.

His words spewed out, getting louder with each syllable. "I told you at our first meeting. You…don't…change…anything! That's not up to you as interim. Don't you listen?"

No one moved. No one cleared a throat; I was the only woman present and my throat was tightly closed. The silence was piercing. By the time I could breathe again, it was time to break for lunch.

"It's his meds. They affect his moods," one clergy explained to me quietly, as we moved out of the room.

I never went back.

They Hunt in Packs

It was not my finest hour.

After they all stomped out of the parish, there were great gaping holes to fill in the leadership: parish warden, liturgical assistant, youth group leader, organist and choir director, the entire contemporary music team, lay reader and chalice bearer. Twelve key people left, plus their family members. In a rural parish, where most were related or had known each other since they were kids, the effect was devastating.

Though, as it turned out, it actually wasn't.

The congregational meeting had come and gone. "What's the real reason for this meeting?" a former church warden asked hours before it was to start. "I have brothers, you know, and we're all strong men and we know how to wield two-by-fours."

"No need for that," I hastily assured him. "The meeting has nothing to do with me."

I told him what I knew and believed. The archdeacon (representing the bishop's authority) and a representative from Church Army would be fielding questions about what had just happened at the church's national meeting and about one controversial issue in particular, the blessing of same-sex unions. It hadn't been approved, despite all rumours circulating to the contrary, but had been put off for further study.

I was wrong.

For months, I had known something in the parish was sideways. But I wasn't sure what. I was still new to the parish, still trying to get to know everyone as their rector, still trying to get my sea legs under me. I watched and listened and tried to make sense of what was going on.

There was the odd comment made during home visits. "Why are you stopping your assistant from doing home communions?"

I wasn't.

Conversations stopped when I dropped into the youth group.

"That's where I sit. Move," the lay reader said the first Sunday I showed up for service. Months later, the relationship wasn't getting any better.

Another worship leader, who had health issues and was wheelchair bound, had been sidelined in the months before I arrived when the parish was without a full-time rector. "He doesn't have the commitment needed to do the work," the liturgical assistant said, when I asked why he wasn't being called upon.

Efforts to introduce new services and to widen the circle of leadership came to nothing.

I found out that the group got together socially, had their own Bible study, and e-mailed each other most days. They had an impressive array of abilities which they offered unreservedly when left on their own. They shared a suspicion of top-down authority, at least of the clerical kind, which was curious since they had originally been raised up from their peers and encouraged in their ministries by a previous rector.

"To be a real leader," one of them patiently explained to me, "you have to have the three 'A's: anointing, ability, authority."

"And who exactly measures that?" I asked.

The large church was packed on the night of the meeting. My archdeacon was chairing, and I sat at the prayer desk close by, perpendicular to the people. We opened in prayer.

It wasn't long before the topic shifted from national church decisions to the local churches. *Had the archdeacon suspected it would take this turn?* I wondered.

Then, one by one, key people from the group made their way forward and stepped up to the microphone on the pulpit. Looking out over the sea of faces, focusing in on their families, they began to speak.

Each pronouncement was much the same. "I can't serve under the present conditions. The new rector holds a position about the blessing of same-sex unions that is contrary to Scripture."

Wait a minute. When had I ever expressed my thoughts about this? How could I when, much to my shame, I was still sorting them out?

"I can no longer be part of the Anglican Church if this is what it stands for. Here's my resignation."

Some offered an exposition of Scripture, which the

archdeacon tried to cut off.

Tears trickled down my cheeks. Thank God for being side-to the people instead of facing them. *Don't wipe them away and draw attention.* A warm pressure rested lightly on my left shoulder. *Oh, God, please help all of us.*

Now I knew what was sideways. Why there had been a heaviness in so many meetings, why there'd been whispering in the corners after services, why there was so little laughter at church socials. This was what a visiting clergy friend had meant when she said, "There is a darkness here. Can't you feel it?"

So, now that it's in the open, how on Earth do we go forward? I wondered. *How do I fix this?*

The meeting was on a Friday night. Sunday morning I found it hard to get out of bed. A cold dread descended on me as I stepped out of the shower and thought about the upcoming service.

"We should have prayer warriors praying around the church during each service," a member of the group had said to me shortly after I arrived in the parish. "Praying that the church be shielded from all evil; that each assault be driven back."

That wasn't my particular theological point of view, so I didn't pay much attention at the time. Now I wondered. *Who had been praying, and for what?*

I got to service early but others were earlier still. The pews were full. The lay reader wheeled up next to me into the sanctuary—a most committed guy after all. Together we looked out over old, worn faces, jostling young families, "middlers" settling in, and toddlers wandering down the centre aisle and standing on pews. Light streamed through the windows and into the sanctuary. It rested everywhere I looked—on the pulpit, font, altar, faces—and for once, there were no shadows.

This wasn't mine to fix, I realized.

A month after they left, their new pastor called me. "You

probably know that some of your parishioners have found a new spiritual home here," he began. "What I would like to know is, do they have any fences they should mend with you and the people there?"

Wise man, I thought.

When Death Comes Calling

It doesn't matter if you've done a hundred funerals or more, stood at countless gravesides and said ancient prayers, or even had more than your own share of family deaths. Each death is something new. That first contact with a grieving family is always a delicate one. So is each of the subsequent meetings. In those moments, you experience the best and worst in people, and maybe that's why I have always liked this part of being a priest. What you see is people being *real*. It takes energy to keep the normal masks on. Death's touch strips them all away.

It is first light and you are gone,
we thought we had longer.

Not Invited

The funeral director was nervous, I could tell. I had known him a few years and had never seen him fidgety before.

He was always the soul of discretion and sensitivity, bending over backward so that families would have a "good" funeral experience. I did that as well, so we got along fine. Two professionals, both trying to do our best.

As I walked into his office, I wondered what was up.

Three women, in their sixties, sat in front of the large mahogany desk. They wanted to discuss their plans for their sister's burial. Mel, the funeral director, had already explained that they'd have to get me onboard if they were to inter her in the church cemetery. He pulled out his leather swivel chair for me, while he perched on one corner of his desk.

"First of all," said the woman closest to me, leaning into my space, "it's a graveside only service. There will be no church service."

Not that unusual a request, I thought.

"And we're putting no time for the service in the papers, just the date. We don't want the other part of the family to show up. They're not invited."

"And who is the other part of the family?" I asked.

They named several individuals who were hard-working, there-every-Sunday, generous people from one of "my" churches. I knew them well. I had not seen these women before, however.

Don't rock the boat. Mel's expression sent a silent message. *Don't say what you're thinking.*

"And why don't you want them invited?" I asked.

A litany of abuse poured out of their mouths. "So they're not invited," the woman closest to me finished.

"And what do I say if they ask me when the service is?" I asked.

"Say whatever you want to, but they're not invited," said the woman sitting in the middle.

"No, they're not," the third one agreed.

Be good. Be generous. Don't rock the boat. Mel's expression and my training were working really hard for a civil outcome.

We set the time and date. On the way home, I dropped in to see the part of the family I knew. I asked if they were aware their family member had died. They were, they said, and asked, "When is the funeral?"

"The thing is, they're only having an interment, and they don't want you there."

"She was a churchgoer most of her life and sang in our church choir. She was actually one of the original members," a granddaughter volunteered. The family began supplying other details of her active church involvement over the decades.

It poured on the day of the interment. We gathered around the casket in the wet, wet grass, a small but determined group: me, Mel, three sisters, one friend. It was difficult keeping our footing on the slight incline. The rain came at us sideways. A friend had written a eulogy for the occasion but no one even close to the reader could hear the words. The rain drummed her out.

No one uninvited showed up.

The next week we held a memorial service at the little church where she had once sung. Her blue choir hat sat on a small white linen-draped table just below the altar steps. The church was crammed with her friends and the rest of the family, with former choir members and some current ones, and anyone else who wanted to be there to remember and celebrate her life.

The announcement in the papers read, "Everyone welcome."

When the Band Played

I pulled the disposable yellow gown over my street clothes and entered the private hospital room. Anyone coming in had to do so because of the risk of infection. Gown and gloves and facemask: they weren't for visitors; they were a protective barrier for the young man lying weakly on the bed. He had just had a bone marrow transplant, which was severely compromising his immune system.

Though he couldn't speak much, or loudly, he hitched his thin frame up a bit in the bed. Using his words sparingly, he explained his disease and his situation. It looked bad, he said, but he was still hopeful.

The conversation drifted eventually to his friends and how much he missed being in the band with them. "They've been so good about keeping me involved, you know. They bring me recordings of their latest songs. We've known each other a long time."

What is "long" to a twenty-year-old?

He died a week later.

My parish church was far too small for all the people expected to come, so arrangements were made to hold the funeral in a large downtown church. I arrived early that day to check out the space and get my bearings.

They were waiting for me at the massive church door: six men, in their early twenties, dressed in suits, ties and gleaming shoes. "Listen," one said, "we have a special request to make. He was member of our band." (I knew that.) "We'd like to play a piece for him during the service. Would it be okay if we did? It would mean a lot to us."

They set up their instruments in front of the church pews, on the other side from where the coffin would sit. Drums, guitars, and mic at the ready. We decided that they would play at the very end of the funeral, just before everyone left for the cemetery.

I didn't ask what piece they would play. Most clergy would have (sometimes things can go sideways if the one responsible for overseeing the service doesn't know what's coming next). I looked at their dress clothes and remembered the stories he had told me about them, and I knew that they had chosen their music carefully and that it would be fine.

The church was packed. It usually is when a young person dies. People of all ages jammed into the long pews and stood several deep along the edges of the large, columned room. Some stood outside in the crisp fall air, listening to the service on speakers.

On cue, at the end of the service, the young men took their places at the front. They played well and with all their hearts. It was a familiar song. *He Ain't Heavy, He's My Brother.* Then they laid their instruments down and moved to the centre aisle. Two abreast, three on each side, they picked up the casket and proceeded out.

Sometimes it's good not to know what's coming next.

Who's to Blame?

I was running on fumes— not a good thing to do when you spend a good part of most days on the road—so I pulled into the closest full-service gas bar. *Might cost a bit more but better safe than sorry.* An attendant walked over, leaned in through the window, and then slowly smiled in a weary kind of way.

She had long, dark hair pulled back in a limp ponytail, and a deeply lined face though she was surely not more than forty. She looked vaguely familiar, though I couldn't quite place her. It was clear, however, that she recognized me. Such is the blessing and curse of being one of the few ministers in a rural area. Everyone knows you and you are expected to know them, their name, and their story.

We exchanged a few pleasantries, and as she kept an eye on the gas pump she volunteered, "We're doing ok. His wife moved out of the area, you know, not too long after you did the funeral. Took the kids with her." It was clear she assumed I knew the circumstances to which she was referring.

"How's she doing?" I asked, desperately trying to piece together the story. I'd done way too many funerals recently; which one was she connected to? The way this conversation was going, I needed to know sooner rather than later.

"Don't know. Don't care. She's gone and that's a good thing.

She moved closer to her family and we don't have to look at her."

She finished pumping and I fished out my card. Why is it so hard to find things even in a small purse? We walked slowly back into the garage. I waited as she rang in the amount, still not sure whom we were talking about.

"What I'd like to know is why didn't she get him some help? She knew he was ill. I knew he was ill. Everyone in the family knew it. She did nothing!" The attendant slammed an oil container down on the counter to emphasize her point.

Ah, I finally had it—this was the sister. I began to recall other details.

It had been a cold winter's day and an even colder wait at the cemetery for the large crowd of people to disperse. No one had wanted to just leave him there, so exposed to the elements.

A single rose was brought to the front of the church by his little son, and carefully laid in front of the urn.

The church was filled with people not usually there, spilling out into the centre aisle.

A tiny woman stood beside me at the door, older looking than her age—35, my records showed—mostly being ignored by members of her husband's family.

Another death in the community, but this time not because of age or car accident or disease (not of the body, anyway). His wife had driven him into emergency just the previous week but he told the doctors nothing was wrong. "They wouldn't keep him over in the psych ward even one night to check him out," she'd said. "Just gave him a pocketful of numbers to phone if he needed to, and sent him home." He'd seemed better that last day, she told me. "The kids and I were going shopping in town. He waved goodbye." Then, he'd walked into the woods behind the house with his gun. "I miss him every day."

"I miss him every day," the attendant said.

Where was he now? I wondered. "In God's hands" was my

standard answer and I believed that. I have witnessed too many things over the years not to believe in a reality beyond this one. But what would that look like? Somewhere out of pain, finally free of the heaviness that had captured him so young, and stripped him of so much? Rotting somewhere in a dark place for having the audacity to say, "Enough!"? Doing penance for all the pain and questions he set in motion that day, which would surely ripple down through the generations? Did he regret his decision? It was his, after all.

"It could have been so different if she had just been paying attention," his sister added.

Blame: it's more energizing than pain, and easier than living with the unanswerable. I knew this. I gave her a hug and drove away.

It Happened in the Hospital

Time is warped in a hospital. So are a lot of other things. Enter those sliding glass doors and you find yourself in an alternate reality.

Nothing prepares you for what might be just around the corner, lying on a stretcher, breathing heavily through a mask, waiting behind the privacy curtain, or sitting at the nurses' station. This is not a place for cowards or for those without a sense of humour, or for uttering platitudes—though those of us who walk its halls have been guilty of all these things at times. The hospital is reality served up on a big stick. Take a taste, see if you like it. It's not for everyone.

Bodily Functions and an Inexperienced Priest

The blue plastic urinal sat squarely in the middle of the only table in the room. The windowsill was filled with flowers. The stand beside the bed overflowed with Kleenex, a pair of reading glasses, a writing pad and pen, paper bags, and magazines. A phone teetered on one end of it.

The narrow table was wheeled up mid-way across the bed, within easy reach of the old man in case he needed it. The nurses were always busy, and who wanted to sit in cold wet sheets waiting for someone to come and *tut, tut* over them for not being able to wait?

The two women from the home communion team looked around the room and didn't know what to do. I, their new priest and supposedly savvy in such matters, didn't either.

The old man had requested Communion, and here we were, but where were we going to set up for it? You know: spread out the white place mat (corporal), lay down the serviette (purificator), place the cup for the wine (chalice) and the plate for the bread (paten).

There was only one place.

Leadership takes nerve, I told myself, *though I didn't expect to be demonstrating it this way.* I gingerly took hold of the blue plastic urinal—oh, dear, it was full—lifted it from its central location, and placed it as far to the right side of the table as I could. Then I asked the team to set up.

And so we celebrated Communion together—the old man and the home communion team from his parish, both of whom he knew well, and me, gathered around a table with evidence of his bodily functions very much on display at one end.

Thinking back, I realize I could have handled the situation so much better. I could have set the urinal on the floor until after the service, with the hope that I wouldn't forget to give it back to him when I left. Or, and maybe this would have been the best solution, I could have emptied the bottle of its warm contents and stuffed it with flowers for the table.

Absolution

I have seen many things happen as someone lies dying in a hospital room. The family gathered around the bed saying goodbye—yes, too many times to count. But this gathering was different.

For one thing, the family hadn't expected to be there. Their dad was only supposed to be in overnight after a routine surgery.

He'd booked in for a simple procedure. Nothing to worry about, he'd told them. And why would they worry? He was in his mid-sixties, a fit man by any measure, and with a great attitude. But something had gone badly wrong in surgery and now here he was, unconscious, and not expected to survive the night.

They were a large family of siblings, eight in all. With their spouses there, too, the tiny ICU room was more than a little crammed. I stepped outside the glassed-in enclosure to give them space and to get a bit of breathing room.

What could I say to them? This was a family of professionals, though right now they were all children, saying goodbye. Platitudes wouldn't be appreciated—are they ever? I watched them through the glass wall as they leaned into each other, held one another up, and passed old stories around. They were accepting this awful situation with grace and humour, facing it full-on and not turning away.

It was here, as I looked in on them, that the surgeon found me. The collar is always a dead give-away. "Look," he said, after introducing himself, "Tell them I'm sorry, would you? It wasn't supposed to happen like this. Please tell them I'm sorry."

"Tell them yourself," I snapped. *My God, we're all on edge here,* I thought.

He looked down at me for a few seconds, considering. Then he squared his shoulders, opened the heavy glass door, and walked in. The family parted as he made his way to the head of the bed. He turned and faced them and began to apologize in a low voice.

They gathered in around him as they had their dad. One son said, "It wasn't your fault. We knew there was a risk with surgery at his age." Another added, "These things sometimes happen. It was just his time." A daughter said, "It must be hard when things go wrong." And then I heard, "Thank you for being here," as heads nodded in agreement.

Never had I witnessed confession such as this (lawsuit be damned, some things that play on a soul are just too heavy) or absolution so beautifully given.

Buns of Steel and Homemade Bread

Sometimes relationships begin in odd ways.

It started in the hospital during my first day on the job as a clergy. When I got the call to come to the ICU as soon as possible, I really hustled, grateful there were no cops patrolling the highway that morning. I remember running across the parking lot, pushing the elevator button several times, and then rushing by a woman crying just outside its doors (*not my concern right now. There's an emergency happening here*, I thought. Yes, there was…more than one in fact.).

I came upon him in the family room, a slim, wiry man in his late sixties named Daniel. He was sitting at one end of the brown plastic sofa, his head in his hands, focusing on nothing—or perhaps on too much.

"Thanks for coming," he said, getting up stiffly and shaking my hand. "It's my wife, Lottie. They want to cut off her legs to save her life. I know they're probably right, but I just don't know if I can do it. She's unconscious now and I can't ask her." He looked extremely tired. His eyes began to water. "What if I'm doing the wrong thing? What would she want? I just don't know."

Daniel and I walked into the unit and stood by her bed. I reached down to take her limp hand and he held my other one. We prayed for a few moments, asking for guidance and deliverance. The equipment continued to beep all around us.

* * *

Some stumps never fully heal. I didn't know this until I met

Lottie. She was home now, and spent her days in a wheelchair. She'd managed rehab well, though the pain from the phantom limbs never went away, and she could not bear standing on her prosthetics.

Their house, a 1940s two-storey located on a little cul-de-sac, was spacious enough to accommodate her chair with only a few modifications. They moved their bed downstairs into a side room just off the kitchen. The move came after weeks of her climbing the stairs each night, one step at a time, on her butt. She commented on how firm she was getting in at least one region and I began calling her Buns of Steel. We wondered together if Jane Fonda had anything on her. It was harder getting back downstairs, she told me.

She was generously proportioned, had thinning brown hair, a smile that never quit, and hands that were always knitting something. Somewhere among my things, I still have a pair of red mittens she made me one Christmas.

I relished my time with them, not only because they were so obviously in sync with each other, but because of their deep faith in a loving God, despite all they had been through. She was Catholic but she knew no priests in the area. Daniel was Anglican, reconnecting now to a church community after several decades' absence. I became their priest and they became my inspiration of how marital vows should be lived.

We set up a schedule of home communions, usually mid-mornings after she'd had time to get herself up and dressed and Daniel had put on the coffee pot. We'd sit at their chrome kitchen table with Communion laid out in front of us on a white tablecloth, passing the wine and bread between us. Afterward, we'd talk of family and friends. We'd discuss challenges, past and current, and their intention to never be a burden to their children. We did so over steaming mugs of really good coffee.

Daniel had once cooked for large groups of people in the

military, he told me, and then added that he missed it. Perhaps that was why he offered to help a men's group at the church with their roast beef dinner each year. His was a much-appreciated skill set and the other men welcomed him with open arms. He became an important part of the team. When he wasn't in the kitchen, he would don a white shirt, black pants and bowtie, and wait on tables. At some point during each dinner, he would go to the side door where the wheelchair ramp fed into the hall, open it, and then carefully and proudly wheel his beloved Lottie in and up to a reserved spot near the front. She always wore something glittery and smart.

* * *

The Scripture that I was to preach on one Sunday was from the Gospel of John: "Jesus said, 'I am the Bread of Life.'" In preparation for the sermon and the Eucharist that day, I picked up a small round loaf from the grocery store and set it on the altar, prominently displayed so that people would notice it. It was such a hit that we switched from wafers to real bread that day and never looked back.

Daniel took notice. Not long afterward, he approached me with an offer to bake the bread for Communion each week. He was adamant that it would be his special offering to the church. So began years of the most delicious bread being brought to the altar each Sunday, and shared with the people at the rail.

It was mouth-watering and light, with just a hint of honey. It seldom crumbled, which was always a concern with real bread, especially when children received at the rail (crumbs dropping everywhere) and when people dipped it into the wine in the common cup (dipping, otherwise known as intinction, was still permitted in those less sanitary-conscious days). The symbolism was more obvious than with the individual wafers, as big generous pieces were broken off at the rail and placed into the hands lifted up to receive: "We are one body, for we share in the one bread." Daniel's bread still comes to mind whenever I say that line in the service. For years, he took joy in being able to offer this gift each week.

One day, just before I was to visit them, I got a call from Lottie. Daniel had gone out for a few minutes, she told me, and she needed to tell me something. "What is it?" I asked, my heart in my throat. Who knew what medical problem was looming? They had handled so many over the last while.

It all spilled out. "He isn't remembering things," she told me. "He's forgetting more and more these days. He tries to cover it up but I know what's happening. He won't listen to me and give up making the bread. He won't. Last week he threw out three batches before he got it right. He won't admit there's a problem. I don't want him embarrassed. Can you speak to him, please?"

How do I ask him to give up something he loves doing so much? What could I say that he would hear without being hurt or feeling betrayed? Please God, help me figure this out.

After Communion that morning, we sat talking around the old chrome table. Daniel enjoyed baseball. He talked about it in the church kitchen, with the men hanging around the kitchen pass-thru, and with various friends at church after service.

"So when should a great ball player retire?" I asked.

Without hesitating, he said, "When he's at the top of his game."

They still talk about his bread in that church. They will tell you it was heavenly.

"Taste and see that the Lord is good, Happy are they that trust in him."

Even the Sparrow

It was the one unit I'd hoped I'd never have to enter. It was at one end of a long corridor, and you had to go through two separate doors before you could see anyone. Between those two doors was a supply of disposable hospital gowns, gloves, masks, and a wash-up station. *Ensure you scrub in the following manner...* read the instruction sheet above the basin.

I had come to see my neighbour who was in the burn unit.

I had known him for several years by then and always wondered how old he was. It was hard to tell from his activity level, but I suspected he was in his early eighties. He was known to be strong, and was often seen walking around on roofs to make sure the work was done right on the houses he had been contracted to construct. He had built my house a few years earlier, based on a design he had hoped to construct for his wife, but she had changed her mind and my family had benefited, big time.

The house was a large sprawling brick-and-cedar bungalow set at the very top of the subdivision, overlooking an inlet of the ocean. There was an open-concept kitchen and family room, and an in-law suite complete with bathroom at the opposite end, far away from our bedroom, perfect for when my mother-in-law came to stay for a week or so at a time. The house was gorgeous, but it was the view of the bay that took my breath away each morning when I stood at the picture window, sipping my coffee.

He had called my mother-in-law Madam any time she was visiting; an odd salutation for such a country man. He was unfailingly courteous to women, and shrewd when dealing with men.

He'd built up his construction business by cutting out the middleman and delivering a good product at a fair price. He knew his bottom line and he wouldn't budge. Most of the houses in the subdivision were his construction, and he had plans to expand further into the tree line above the bay. "Don't tell him he's getting old; just try keeping up with him on any worksite," his sons said.

It was a freak accident. He'd insisted on checking the equipment himself, had lowered himself down into the pit, lit a match, and that was it.

I stood scrubbing up between the doors, my heart beating faster by the moment. *It's not about you,* I told myself. *Just do it!* Why was I so afraid?

The nurse just inside the second door walked me to the entrance of a small, private room. The room was dimly lit, machinery beeped rhythmically, and the bed moved up and down like some great sleeping beast, air pumping in and out, adjusting to its burden. Nestled in the very centre was something shrunken and tiny, hooked up to tubes and oxygen.

I stepped into the dimness, step by slow step, and approached the breathing bed. Was this the right room? There was a lot of equipment hooked up to him. I didn't recognize what I could see of the patient.

I looked down at his face. I remembered my six-year-old son bringing a tiny baby bird to me that had dropped out of a nearby nest. It had no feathers yet, just pink, pink skin stretched thinly over bone, rising and falling with each breath. Together we had placed it gently beneath some fuchsia-coloured Impatiens in the back yard, so its last glimpse would be of beauty. *Do birds this tiny see?* I had wondered.

I knew I couldn't touch my neighbour. Instead, I began to softly tell him stories about what an amazing house he had imagined and then built...how he had cared for my family that first winter when the pipes froze and some valves didn't work right...how my heart still sang looking out over the bay...the memories I and my husband and our son were making now, in that beautiful place.

Oh, Crap!

There are some in every profession: people who shouldn't be there. They either lack the skills, or the temperament, or both. They don't like what they're doing but for some reason they keep showing up to work.

One memory, from too many years ago to count, keeps popping up sometimes when I do my hospital visits. I was a student ward aid at a small country hospital. It was one of the few summer jobs a girl aged sixteen could get in a small town. It was hard work and it changed how I viewed hospitals and the people who work there day in and day out.

Alice didn't want to be a ward aid. She was solidly built, a woman of about forty or so, with a mouth that just wouldn't smile. Most of the other ward aids had a great sense of humour, but not Alice. I knew nothing about her background or family circumstances, and that might have explained much. All I knew was that I didn't like working with her.

Sometimes Alice was the one in charge of the junior ward aids (like me) for a few shifts. My heart would drop when the weekly schedule came out and I'd see our names in the same time block. It wasn't that Alice was mean to me, or unreasonable. It was just that she didn't treat some of the patients very well.

She especially didn't like the psychiatric patients who came in and stayed for months. There was no psychiatric facility within a hundred miles of us, and when someone got particularly hard to handle at home and the family doctor agreed to it, the hospital got a new admission.

Like Harold. He had a bed on the public four-person ward, and he talked a lot but not in words anyone could understand. Sometimes his hand shook so badly, he couldn't feed himself.

My job, like Alice's, was to help out on the wards—making beds, giving bed baths, freshening up patients before the end of shift with a warm hand cloth and soapy water, feeding them if they couldn't feed themselves, emptying urinals and bedpans, and so on.

One day I walked into the ward and Alice was leaning over Harold. She was shoving him roughly over on his side as she began to change the bed. Then she slammed him back down, and shoved him up on his other side to finish. "Why do you always wet the bed just after a shift begins? My shift begins? Stupid, stupid man," she muttered. Harold didn't know much about what was going on that day. He just lay there, trying to make himself small. She stalked out.

I thought that Harold was quite smart, actually. I'd seen the comment he had made a few days earlier on the hospital food.

That particular day, Harold was having a good day and insisted on feeding himself. I started him off just to be sure he wasn't shaking too much, then left him alone as he ate. I went in later to pick up his tray, which he had reassembled. When the kitchen crew downstairs removed the lid from his dinner plate, they found, neatly laid in the centre of the plate, one large, nicely-formed turd. How he managed to get it there, I have no idea.

Later, the same afternoon of the bed-slamming incident, Alice walked into the ward again. This time she was intent on picking up the garbage. There was one sink in each ward, and a garbage pail sat under the sink. A large plastic bag protected the insides.

I knew what Alice would do next: lift it out with one hand in one smooth motion (she was a strong woman), twirl it around at chest level, and tie it up.

I was preparing to empty it myself, using an entirely different method; I just had to get Harold back into bed first.

She got there first. She picked up the large, heavy plastic bag, held it at chest level, and began twirling it around. It burst in two places right along the seam, spraying her pristine, white ward aid uniform from top to bottom with urine and turd.

In any hospital, most people who attend to the sick, the dying, or the mentally ill are compassionate, dedicated, gentle yet firm, and hard-working. Most have a great sense of humour, care deeply about their patients, and are a credit to their profession.

Then there are the others like Alice. Behind the privacy curtains, in the hallways, pushing a wheelchair or stretcher, I sometimes hear them trying to make a patient feel small. I want to take them aside and say, "Go home, give it up, and do something you really want to do. Something that will bring you joy. Do it now before your attitude catches up with you. Let me tell you about Harold."

The Nature of Shame

There have been too many moments when I haven't listened to the promptings of my heart.

Red always sat twelve pews down, left-hand side, wedged into the tight space with his best friend Charlie and Charlie's wife, Marge. He was a big man, standing well over six feet, in his late seventies at the time we first met, with a full head of thick white hair, deep blue eyes, and a pale complexion. He was known as Red, perhaps a nod to his younger years and Irish roots. He'd listen to you and you'd know you were being heard.

Sundays he went to church, Wednesdays he drove widows to doctor's appointments or to the grocery store in his old silver Cadillac. Tuesdays and Thursdays, he'd spot off his friend Charlie for a few hours and sit with Marge, who was slowly succumbing to cancer.

She'd talk and talk. They'd been friends for years. He would just listen and smile. Try to pick out the odd phrase against the growing silence in his ears.

We got on well. I'd speak loudly and he'd adjust the hearing aid and focus in. He'd tell me about the neighbourhood and church in former days, about his family, gone now, about the dream he used to have of going back to the Emerald Isle. We'd laugh some, ponder some. We'd say a prayer, one he remembered from his childhood, and promise to get together again soon. I looked forward to visits with him.

The last few months, Red had been spending more and more time in the regional hospital. "Wrecks my schedule," he complained. Something was wrong but the doctors couldn't diagnose it.

The call from the hospital came in at the end of an evening meeting and a long day. Such calls always seemed to come in when I was bone-tired. Another parishioner had been admitted and wanted to speak to me.

It was nine o'clock when I walked through the front doors of the hospital, hit the elevator button and rode up to the third floor. The elevator opened onto a place radically different from the daytime. It was quiet now, the constant hum of machines and voices and hospital busyness subdued. Lights were dimmed in the halls and out in the patients' rooms, except for the night-lights. I was directed to a bed closest to the window in the four-person ward. Curtains were drawn around it, giving the illusion of privacy.

We talked, me and the man in the bed, of family, of past church association, of his experiences of God. We laughed some and he cried some. He was not dying but afraid; not in pain, but hurting. We said the Lord's Prayer together, his words half a beat behind mine. I left him with a blessing and a promise to return.

Red is somewhere here tonight, I thought, as I pressed the elevator button. *I should find out where and drop in.* Instead, I said a quiet prayer for him and headed home.

First thing in the morning, the hospital called again. "Someone from your parish has died," they said. I was refreshed now, ready to be there in any way I could for the grieving family. I checked in at the nurses' station, made my way in the morning light to the room, pushed back the curtains that were pulled around the bed, as they usually are after a death in a ward.

The body was laid out, ready for family viewing and priestly ministrations. I moved closer. I hadn't recognized the name when they called, just absorbed the phrase, *one of yours*. Same room as last night, the bed next to the one I had sat beside. How odd to be here again for someone else. I looked down. Red. *Oh God, dear friend.*

Did you hear my voice, the laughter and the prayers, drifting through the curtains last night?

Or did the silence of your ears drown out everything? Like the tiredness had silenced my heart?

The Sacredness of Buildings

It has taken me most of my life to understand the attachment people have to church buildings. Maybe it's because I moved around a lot, even as a child. It was too hurtful to give my heart to some special place knowing that sometime up ahead I'd be leaving.

For me, church has always been the people: the fellowship and brokenness of believers, and those who want to believe. The building was just the place where the people, with whom I loved and struggled, gathered. Take the physical structure away, and the church would still carry on. I'm baffled by the concept of one particular place where God, who created micro- and macro-cosm, universes within universes, is focused. I do admit, though, that I've encountered that all-enveloping presence at rail and altar, in the nave (where the congregation sits), in meeting halls, and in noisy Sunday School classes.

Now, finally, I understand a little about why people have such a difficult time when a church building is changed even a bit, and why grief overwhelms so many when the doors close for the last time.

Pews are emotional connections to grandparents, to friends we have sat beside on Sunday mornings. That honour roll on the wall just inside the door has the name of the young uncle I never met. The bell that came crashing down and almost took out the ringer, the one that sat on the church lawn for a decade, can't just be shoved away in the back of someone's garage. It needs a tower, even if we don't know how to pay for it yet.

Rearranging the Furniture

I arrived early on the morning of the Great Reveal, long before the first service was to begin. I wanted to check out the new arrangement. As I walked to the back of the church and looked forward, I realized that I had probably made a big mistake. This was only my second year here and I was already making major changes to the church space. In theological school, we were taught not to act too quickly, to get the lay of the land and the trust of the people first. I remembered that now. Too late.

It was all part of my plan to make more room for the expanding music ministry, and to be closer to the people. In the previous weeks, I had quietly been checking this out with key members of the congregation.

The altar had been pulled out from the wall years before; glad I hadn't had to fight that battle! It now sat at least twenty feet closer to the people, at the top of the one step leading up from the congregation. Behind the altar, to each side, were the choir seats. The pews had disappeared, and movable seats were now arranged behind wooden frontals, to camouflage legs and speaker cables and books. The organ was no longer in front of the first pew in the congregation where the organist always sat with his back to the people, trying to maintain a ramrod posture throughout the services. It was now tucked into a front corner of the church sanctuary, facing the choir. "I can finally relax," the organist said, grinning. A cobbled-together rail ran across the front of the rearranged space, some hinges making up the difference in span from its former location.

A whole lot of shocked people were beginning to arrive, looking up now and then at the changes, but not meeting my eyes.

It was now two minutes to the start of service. Two minutes before I'd have to explain myself. Two minutes that seemed to stretch out much longer, as I watched the community gathering in silence instead of the normal laughter and greetings.

One minute to service and with everyone settled in, Corienna stood up.

Corienna was a tiny, white-haired, lovely looking woman in her eighties. The people, without exception, loved her. Many remembered her standing at the church doors years before with her beloved husband, welcoming them into the church on their first Sunday. She was soft-spoken, gentle, and gave big bear hugs. She sat each Sunday in the front right pew, beside a stained glass window that featured an angelic harp. Here she had sat with her husband, with her children. Now she sat with a dear friend who liked music, too. On a sunny day, when the sunlight streamed in, it seemed to glow especially brightly around Corienna.

Corienna drew up every inch of her four-foot-ten frame. She turned, faced me, and said in a clear, loud voice (she who usually spoke so quietly), "Oh! Reverend Bonnie, I'm so pleased! This is beautiful!" She looked around at the new space. "And now that the organ's moved, I can finally see the altar from my seat!" She sat down.

The service began. No one said anything negative about the new space that day. Most never did.

Blessings come in many forms.

Room to Swing a Casket

All the research had been done, the aesthetically-gifted consulted, the council's approval secured. Only one step remained: make sure the congregation knew what was coming next.

Getting this far had been a struggle. Who would have thought taking out two pews at the back of the church, pews that were used only rarely, would create such a fuss?

I had done my best for a year to convince council it would be a good idea, and then I had given up.

How do you counter, "Don't ask me to help with it. I was part of removing pews to make room for the stairwell and you wouldn't believe how upset people got. I'm not going through that again."

Or, "It'll cost too much. We can't pay our regular bills now."

Or, "Why do we need a space up here for coffee hour? We have a great hall downstairs."

"People won't go downstairs if they're new. Even most regulars won't," I explained patiently. "It's easier to go out those doors and home. But if they have to walk through people having coffee at those doors, they might just stay."

"They can come downstairs."

I dropped the idea. Then some new members of council took up the challenge. One of them was in charge of the music and people listened to him. *Don't want to risk doing without music, do we?* I thought uncharitably. One council meeting, not long afterward, they all ended upstairs, measuring out how much space would be freed up and where they could put the plugs for coffee. Suddenly it was a go again.

The next Sunday, I decided to incorporate the information about the soon-to-be created social space into my sermon, connecting it to the Word of the Day and to the mission of the church. Just as I said, "And that's the plan, so don't be upset when you come in next week and find the back looking different," a woman stood up. A member of council.

Bet you there's no "Amen, sister, preach it!" comment coming, I thought.

"Excuse me, Reverend, but you can't rip those pews out. The

fire marshal will shut us down."

When was the last time I've been part of an interactive sermon? I thought.

The place, never that noisy unless the children were upstairs, went dead quiet. It felt like people were holding their breath. Maybe I was the only one doing that.

The woman continued, "You'll be breaking fire regulations. All those people gathered at the door. What if we had an emergency?"

This is an emergency, my inner sensors warned. *Got to concentrate really hard now…critical to demonstrate calm, cool leadership under fire* (no pun intended).

I took her points one by one and dealt with them right then in the middle of the sermon. People were shifting uncomfortably.

"Clearly," I said to everyone, "more discussion is needed on this matter. But this isn't the place to do it."

The service limped forward, and didn't recover its balance even with Communion.

The organist and the other council members who supported the proposed new space were visibly upset. Others looked vindicated. It was a mess.

I preached on community the next Sunday. Few of the vindicated ones were there. But I preached anyway. The message was, "How can we be welcoming to newcomers when we can't even get along with each other?" I had no idea how to go forward.

But some sitting in the pews did. They already had council's approval.

They called me after the deed was done. The pews were flipped around so they faced into the new space, a rug covered the marred floor, and a long table donated from another church stretched along one side. It was a beautifully spacious area now, with plenty of room for people to move away from the door, sit down and talk to one another or get to know someone new.

Someone put a hundred dollar bill on the offering plate to cover any expenses. There were none. They didn't have to ask for help from those who had removed pews before.

A while later there was a funeral in the church. The funeral director showed up well beforehand as he always did. "Wow!" he said, looking around at the new space. "Lots of room to swing a casket!"

Not in Vain

It was a testy meeting. How could it be otherwise, considering what we were discussing?

I had been warned what to expect by my regional dean (bishop's administrator in the region) and by the rector of the parish. Now I sat beside them at the front of the low-ceilinged conference room, facing about twenty people from two church councils. The purpose of the meeting? That appeared to depend on who was speaking.

"You won't have to do anything," the regional dean had told me. "Just be a calming presence as their archdeacon."

The meeting began with a prayer, introductions, and a slide show detailing the sad state of one of the churches. "This is why the bishop has written your wardens that worshipping in the building is prohibited," the regional dean explained. "It's dangerous. Until such time as the problems are corrected, it's unusable. As you can see, the damage is extensive."

The engineering consultant, who had assessed the building and prepared the slides, fielded a few questions from both councils. It was obvious a lot of money would be needed if that particular church were ever to reopen.

The agenda was beginning to sort out in my mind.

One council was talking about how and when to shut down their church building. It was in much better repair than the one in the slide show, though they just couldn't make a go of it financially any longer. The decision to close had obviously already been made, and their members seemed at peace with it. They were anxious to know when exactly the bishop could come and deconsecrate the building, and what they needed to take care of leading up to that. The process was far more complicated than they had anticipated, I noticed, yet they were still game. One of the members took detailed notes as her warden asked clarifying questions.

The other council was largely quiet. *Still trying to absorb the slide show*, I thought. One large man in his fifties was sitting in the front row of his council, his arms folded across his chest. He seemed to be set on simmer.

"We can fix this," he said finally in a loud voice, waving one hand at the projector. "People are missing their church. *I'm* missing my church. If the diocese would let us keep more of our money we'd have enough." This was a direct reference to the allotment each church is required to pay. Councils always, I noticed, alluded to this when their church was hurting financially.

"If we had a student minister," he said, not looking at his rector, "he could go out and bring more young people in." Attracting young people was the eternal challenge, I thought, and most people didn't consider their rector up to the task.

So, I thought. *There it is. A different agenda entirely. Not When and How, but If.*

This man was obviously a leader, perhaps their warden. Heads were nodding all around him as he spoke. How would the regional dean and rector handle this?

The questions hung in the air. But then, how do you respond to largely rhetorical questions? How do you try to address such barely concealed anger? And why is it always the rector and the diocese that are blamed when a church closes?

* * *

I recalled sitting in a large country kitchen in a home beside the Bay of Fundy, another time, another province. I was there to discuss a wedding with a young couple. The parents of the bride-to-be were sitting in too, perhaps because it was their home. I had, as was often the case with weddings, never seen any member of the family at church.

The meeting went well overall until I was standing at the door about to leave. It's always at the door that the bombshells hit.

"So will you tell me just why you had to demolish our church?" the mother asked, completely out of the blue. *You…demolish… our church…* Fragments flew at me, hitting their target.

"How long has it been your church?" I asked.

"It's always been the family church," she answered.

The church hasn't been open for regular worship for more than fifty years. The congregation simply disappeared. So define family church, I thought.

"We would have made a donation to keep it open, you know," the dad said. "But no one asked."

Right. We're going to go door to door in these communities when there's no longer even a church list of past parishioners on the off chance that we'd collect enough money to keep a building open when there is no congregation left.

"The bigger question," I heard myself say, not quite succeeding in holding my tongue, "is how many more churches are going to close because no one goes to them anymore? They're not museums, you know."

They asked another clergy to do the wedding.

* * *

I plummeted back to the present with the thought: *Rectors and the diocese, the bishop, and councils, they are all easy targets.*

Ah…now it's clear. This council knows they will have to shoulder some of the blame whatever they do.

The rector, the regional dean, and the engineer excused themselves to go over to the main church for a few minutes on another urgent matter. It introduced a little space into a taut time.

I stayed with the people, still sitting at the front table. An unexpected silence descended. Looking at the crossed arms, slumped shoulders, and upset faces, I heard myself say, "You haven't failed, you know." *Where had that thought come from?*

Several heads lifted. The man's arms sagged.

"You've kept both churches going this long. You haven't let down those who went before you. You've done good work, which has affected generations. It won't be wasted."

When the threesome returned to the table some time later, the atmosphere in the room was different. Slightly lighter, I thought. Or maybe it was just my imagination.

At the door, as he was leaving, the big man said to me, "Everyone talks about process. You're the first who's talked about how we are feeling."

Only later did I realize that I should have added, "Your rector and regional dean are attending to a thousand other things around this issue. They've been quietly praying for you. Pray for them, would you?"

Last Service

The crispness of the autumn air followed me into the church. It was a bright, clear afternoon, and sunlight streamed through the stained glass windows. It wasn't a large space, but it felt like a home, comfortable and well cared for. There was a warmth in the atmosphere, despite the draught.

How long has it been since the place was so full? I wondered. So many churches were closing in the diocese, city as well as rural ones like this one. Too few people attended, making it impossible to cover building maintenance, let alone pay for ministries or outreach. The result was predictable, and gut-wrenching.

One local contractor bidding on a job at my church had recently asked, "Why would I give the church a break on my costs? The government pays for it, right?" Wrong. Did people not know that churches stood on their own financially or failed? The only sources of income were what came in on the offering plate plus rentals and fundraisers and, if you were so blessed, an occasional benefice. Most regular churchgoers didn't know that unless they took a turn serving on council.

As I sat there looking around, it was hard not to think about the past. For one hundred and fifty-seven years, people had come through these doors, knelt in prayer before service like I just did, picked up a worn prayer book and hymnal and joined their voices with others, thanking and beseeching and confessing. For all those years people had gathered here in laughter and pain, gossiping and caring and trading stories, planning projects, sharing.

How many ministers and students had preached from that raised pulpit? Did their words make any difference at all to those listening? Did they shape values, challenge pious assumptions, touch the hearts of those longing for some answers or comfort?

I was only a visitor, present because I had never been to such a service before, present because I wanted to support the rector on a difficult day. I did not know the stories of the current folk who loved the place—the ones who made the trek for the service, and the ones unable to come but who were thinking about the church. I knew even less about the history of the building and its past congregations and clergy.

Since its beginnings, how many tiny hands had splashed in the baptismal font, how many old wrinkled brows smoothed out the moment the sign of the cross was made on them? How many marriages began at that rail, as the priest's stole was wrapped around a couple's hands, and vows were made before their families, friends, and God? How many people, solitary in grief, followed a casket down the little aisle out into the cemetery surrounding the church? On a Christmas Eve, or early on a Sunday morning, could some people still feel the presence of those long since passed on, worshipping with them?

For more than a century and a half, the church had been *thin space*, as the Celts would say. It had the dimension of a place where the veil between the temporal and the eternal is especially thin; where a person might catch glimpses now and then of something so beautiful it takes the breath away. Is that what I was experiencing sitting there?

The service began. The bishop led the people in prayer. The ancient organ was doing its best, as was the choir (not quite as old). Old voices singing old hymns rose like incense. There were no children. The bread was taken and broken and blessed and handed out. The wine was offered from the common cup one last time at the rail.

The bishop's message echoed in my head. She spoke about the real church: the people, taken by God *(each of us called by name)*,

and broken *(aren't we all somehow?)*,

and blessed *(by this place too)* and given to others. Only the building was being deconsecrated. Not the people. It was a good message.

I walked down the front steps, turned to look back.

We all need something tangible pointing to that which words cannot express, whether it be a sunset or a building, I thought, and then remembered *Everything has a lifespan, including a building.*

Taking Down a Church

As rector, I was due back today after taking a short break. It'd been a tough go in recent months. I was now driving down that part of the highway where I could look off to the left and see the peninsula where the church sat, out past all the salt-water marshes. I shouldn't have been able to see the steeple anymore peeking out above the trees. My warden had assured me the church would be down by the time I got back. I could still see the steeple.

What I wouldn't give to walk away from it all, I thought. This is how it should have gone, in the best of all worlds:

1. Get hired and set derelict church as top priority on my TO DO list.

2. Research old files regarding said church, get to know the players: who wants what done and when.

I had been hired in part because I had promised to do what former rectors hadn't done, which was do something about St. Thomas. I had set it as a top priority and I had done all the necessary background research with a great deal of help from my wardens. I got to know the players: Thorne, the man who wanted to buy the church for a dollar and turn it into a community centre; the once-burnt-twice-shy council members who had been part of deconsecrating and selling another parish church a decade before; the warden who despised public criticism; the warden who would make sure any job was done well for as little as possible.

It was the mother church in the parish. At one time, there had been five churches here. Now there were only two active ones.

The new owners of one church that had been deconsecrated ten years ago kept the steeple, so people still thought of it as a church whenever they drove by. As the fortunes of the owners waned, the building fell into disrepair. Each time I drove home from the city, I saw it sitting there, on a little cul-de-sac just off the highway, mid-point on my journey. It was an enduring reminder to all, that once you sell a building, you lose all control over what happens to it.

3. Check out the church building. Get regional dean to come out and make his recommendations as a former structural engineer.

St. T's was a beauty, at least from the outside. Built almost two hundred years before, it soared into the sky, a lofty wooden edifice with two great oak doors folding into each other, and a brass weather vane in the shape of a whale at the top of the steeple. Graves and tombstones surrounded it on three sides, some almost touching the church walls.

People hadn't worshipped there regularly for almost fifty years. Some rectors and councils had attempted to attract people back to it, but met with little success. Except for the odd summer service, the place had been sealed shut with no heat for decades. That had only accelerated the damage.

The first interview with the local TV station showed an attractive silver-haired man named Thorne standing outside the church.

The interview happened within days of council's decision to reject his request to take over the church. He couldn't show how he was going to finance its maintenance. Council had learned its lesson well with the previously deconsecrated church.

The reporter asked why the council had decided to pull the church down. Thorne said he had no idea why such a travesty was about to take place—look at what good condition the building was in.

When the regional dean and I first ventured past the locks, we encountered black mold growing up the walls in the basement, bat droppings everywhere, tapestries hanging in ribbons, old choir gowns, and prayer books and hymn books left to mold in dusty cupboards and on pew ledges. Plaster was falling from the ceiling; window mouldings disintegrated to the touch. The regional dean said he'd prepare his report on the stability of the building and a slide show indicating problem areas.

The cameraman even managed to take some shots inside, though I didn't know how he avoided the falling plaster, mold, and droppings. Local papers began carrying regular stories on the church, the council and their decision, and their apparent disregard for local sentiment.

4. Present wardens, then council with findings, ask for suggestions. Have a few recommendations in mind. Get their approval on moving forward.

All the public attention played havoc with council. Most members were leaning toward pulling the building down. This was after understanding the church's condition—some actually did a walk-through; all had seen the slideshow—and realizing it would cost well over $100,000 to make it safe enough for worship. The trouble was, they didn't know where they were going to get the money to tear it down, either. Estimates were rather steep; the proximity of the tombstones to the building made the work especially difficult. Some council members were worried about image and how they were already being portrayed in the press. "Can you imagine if we go ahead?" they said.

5a. If council votes to leave the building standing, make sure insurance covers potential liabilities.

There were traces of someone building small fires and having parties in the building. Fortunately, nothing had happened and no one had been hurt so far.

A deciding factor for council seemed to be an image left with everyone at the end of a particularly contentious meeting. Someone said, "We have a responsibility to the church, you know. The corpse is lying on top of the ground, rotting, and we should give it a decent burial."

5b. If council votes to demolish building, get bishop's approval, set date for deconsecration, advise congregations, figure out where funding for demolition is coming from.

Thorne managed to get a reprieve from the bishop's office. Despite council finally approving the demolition and writing to request the bishop's approval, the bishop asked them to reconsider. They did so and reached the same conclusion. Their tolerance of church hierarchy and procedure was getting thinner with every meeting. For the first time in my career, I felt caught between my bishop and the people. *Why does it have to be so complicated?* I thought.

6. Have church deconsecrated by bishop.

De-consecration: the making ordinary of something that has been part of those sacred transitions in people's lives. With this act, the bishop pronounced the building no longer a church. No media showed up to the brief service, just a handful of required witnesses.

7. Proceed with tearing down building, removing debris, landscaping site.

All the bad press had brought the church to the attention of a local contractor. *God does work in mysterious ways, sometimes by means of the awful,* I thought. The contractor specialized in taking down church buildings of a certain sort—and St. T's was of that sort—and reassembling them as homes and cottages somewhere else. He phoned me and made his proposal. I knew my money-conscious warden would be pleased.

And that's how the final pieces fell into place. The contractor agreed to bring down the building without disturbing any adjacent graves, to remove all building materials, grade up the site, and seed it. He offered a modest sum for the privilege. Those monies would eventually be used to erect a large stone memorial on the spot the front doors had once opened into the church.

Upon closer inspection, the contractor found dry rot all through the roof area: so much for rebuilding it elsewhere or for renovating it for use as church again.

On the day of the demolition, I pulled into the lower lot, just below the church. The building was more than half-gone. I noticed two women sitting in a station wagon, a mother and daughter with a history stretching back seventy years and more in this church. They were crying.

I should really go talk to them. My stomach clenched.

Funny how even the awful phone messages left here and there through the past months hadn't bothered me much. It was the nature of the beast. But this moment was something else. This was pure grief for something tangible that would soon be gone in all but memory.

The noise got louder all around them; the sound of boards giving way, walls beginning to crumble. How many mothers had held their children's hands as they walked up those steps the first day of Sunday School?

"We considered tying ourselves to the crane or standing in front of it at one point. But what could two frail women do?" the daughter told me, weeks later.

I walked over to the driver's window and asked how they were. Stupid question. They couldn't look at me. They sat there, staring at the ripping and tearing apart taking place in front of them. I stood beside the window and said a silent prayer. We all stayed until the church was down.

Reclamation

Nothing was marked here. I hadn't seen a road sign or a house for a good half hour, just the odd pull-off along the green river that meandered to my right. It was only 8:30 in the morning and it was already hot. I leaned forward over my Beetle's steering wheel, pulling my sticky back away from the cloth. The road seemed to be getting narrower by the mile. Light slanted in at me through the trees.

I rounded a bend and abruptly everything ended. Road became lumpy field. Grave markers lay directly ahead of my bumper, stuck out at odd angles, some lying on the ground. There, on my left, was the church I had been trying to find. A few other vehicles, mostly trucks, were pulled up beside it. Brooms and a chainsaw and garbage bags poked out of a box on one open tailgate.

This is the fifth church they talk about, I thought. *All the way back here.* It was at least forty kilometers in from where I'd left pavement. I got out of my Bug slowly, taking in the red stonework of the building and steeple, the old oak doors, the fir and hardwood leaning in all around me. How old was this place?

As I entered, I noticed clear glass windows and a potbellied stove in the centre of the room. Already the crew of ten was working hard, sweeping and rearranging. Flies littered the floor, inches deep in places. There was dust and curled up tinsel, dried reddish remnants of fir boughs, and a couple of bulletins from the last service…six months before.

"See our stained glass window?" The woman in charge of overseeing the cleanup pointed to a small, three-foot square piece of artwork framed in pieces of barn board and mounted above the dark wooden altar. It had a dove taking to the air, an olive leaf in its beak. Unbroken water stretched below it. "Harry found that in a chicken coop a few years ago. No idea where it came from or who made it. Cleaned it up and it looks great up there, doesn't it?"

Harry smiled at me as he dumped a dustpan of flies into a garbage bag.

All my questions and more were answered as I pitched in to help get the place service-ready.

"We open the church this time of year every year. Hold a service each month in the summer. There's always a big picnic in

August. Sorry you won't be here for that." The woman in charge of this assembly of cleaners was keen to fill me in.

Here for a good time, not a long time, I thought, remembering my interim status.

"There's homemade lemonade, potato salads, pies, ice cream. Lots of people bring their kids," she continued.

"You should really come back for the service in December, though," someone interrupted. "That's the big one. We all get together a few days before and do what we're doing now, except there's a fair amount of shovelling, too." Obviously, the road was plowed out even in winter weather.

I imagined drifts piling up outside the doors, shifting shape in the winds; a rather nice thought in this heat.

"Then we go to town decorating the church with boughs and candles," said dustpan man.

Lots of fir around here. They probably just go out and cut some at the back of the property, I thought.

"Got to have lots of candles. There's no electricity here, you know," he added.

No heating or light bills either, I mused.

"We get the stove ready to go and Christmas Eve it's something else. People come from all around. Some as far away as Trenton." The town was fifty kilometers away.

Another woman wielding a dust cloth said, "We have cider warming on the stove and all sorts of shortbreads and other cookies. And people stay for a while, slow down a bit before going home."

Now that the altar had been wiped down, someone was unpacking the linens. Then they took the rest of the liturgical hardware out of a box they'd brought. The woman in charge set out the silver chalice and paten on the altar cloth, placed the carafe of wine and boxed wafers on a tiny bare wooden side table, and readied the missile book for me.

I got my gown from the Bug, slipped it over my working jeans and T-shirt, adjusted the cincture, and placed my stole around my neck. I paused just a moment before walking through the glistening clean nave and into the sanctuary, looked up at the reclaimed chicken coop window now filtering bright sunlight. Rainbows scattered across the white linens.

It will always be here, I thought. *So long as there are people who know what moments like this are worth.*

"The Lord be with you," I began.

Let's Start a Rumour

I had two signs that I alternated putting out on the rectory lawn. I had ordered them from an online company and when they came, they were much smaller than expected. However, they could still be seen quite well from the sidewalk.

One was pastoral. Against a backdrop of footprints on a sandy beach, it said, *God loves you. Pass it on.*

The other wasn't. Against a night sky lit up by lightning strikes, it said: *Gossip kills. Don't pass it on.*

Starting and passing on rumours was a regular pastime in my small community. Maybe it was like that in any village. On my more generous days, I thought people didn't appreciate the damage they did; how quickly a small offhand comment could snowball into something too big to control. I'd seen people's lives changed because of a small piece of malicious gossip. People shunned. People labelled forever in their neighbours' eyes.

I knew what that was like, having been the subject of speculation more than once with my colleagues. I remembered how silence would descend abruptly as I walked into a clergy gathering. How no one said anything directly to me but I knew what was being put around. The rumours had spread out like a fast-moving cancer after the past parish blow-up. No one bothered to check out what had happened with me; they'd just accepted the stories at face value. It had been a devastating, wilderness time.

Nothing went unnoticed in a small town, I knew, but sometimes the watchers reached the wrong conclusions. That truck parked overnight at the local tavern. The two spouses of different people meeting for supper at the local eatery. What was the real story? Better still, why speculate at all?

On my cynical days, I suspected some people just liked starting rumours for the power it gave them to be "in the know" and for the sport of watching someone squirm under public scrutiny. No one ever considered that someday they might be the subject of the latest speculation. Preaching about it had absolutely no impact. "Do not bear false witness against your neighbour" was often countered with, "But, pastor, it's true." Didn't they know that gossip damages two souls? The one talked about, and the one doing the talking.

What I really wanted for the front lawn was one of those huge white illuminated signs for different messages. One just as large as some of the local churches had. Maybe larger.

Instead of *Church Roast Beef Supper Saturday, 2-4 pm, $8 adults, $4 children*, it might say, *Did you know all gossipers go to hell? It's in the Bible*. And not give the Biblical reference, which would drive some people crazy.

It could respond to the most current rumours: *The rector is not moving to Norway. Sorry!*

The rectory is not being sold. Unless you make us an offer we can't refuse.

St. M's is not being torn down. It's getting a facelift. Want to be part of the makeover?

I imagined, *Watch this spot for positive rumours* shining brightly into the night. Perhaps that could be the springboard for praising good deeds…

Did you hear that someone in this community:
organized a food bank drive?
drove a neighbour to the doctor?

volunteered to supervise school children at noon hour?
planted flowers in the village square?
shovelled a neighbour's driveway?
visited someone lonely in hospital?
didn't pass on a rumour?

Maybe people would see themselves up there and feel appreciated. Maybe they'd look at each other and wonder.

I imagined more and more people passing by the rectory sign to see the newest posting. It would better than Facebook for those who couldn't manage a computer, like the majority of seniors in the area. Easier to change than the church website. As good as Twitter, with the same spatial restrictions. Short message: more impact.

Until I could afford it, or talk the parish into it, however, I knew I had to be content with my two more generic, little signs. *Time to change them out,* I thought, as I crossed the lawn.

The Minister Doesn't Visit

I made the oddest discovery that summer.

It happened as I went door to door in my capacity as the parish's pastoral visitor, sat in country kitchens sipping tea, and opened conversations designed to get to know the person across the table. The subject of ministerial visits kept coming up. Sometimes it was in response to my question, "Do you have any concerns about the church?" Or as a parting remark at the door, my hand warmly clasped in theirs as they offered it. Sometimes it surfaced in the middle of a conversation as though it had just been waiting for release. "The minister doesn't visit."

At first, I didn't know what to do. Pass the question on to my rector? Keep it to myself? Believe it? *Best make a clean breast of it,* I thought. *Report it and let it go.* It was beginning to shape my opinion of my minister.

"Ah," said my rector. "Interesting. I was just there last week. I dropped in to see how they were doing. That obviously didn't count. Who else did you mention had the same comment?"

People apparently had different definitions of what constituted a visit from the minister. For some, it wasn't a visit if the minister just dropped in, without calling first; showed up late; was there for home communion (that was scheduled); didn't stay for tea; dropped off anything from the church—newsletter, envelopes, invitations.

Emergency calls weren't visits. A follow-up to a funeral wasn't a visit. Initial visits for baptisms or weddings weren't visits. A hospital visit wasn't a visit, it was expected.

It was a complaint I would hear over the years after I was priested. Mainly it was about others. But I could only imagine how many times it was said about me. I'd always hesitate, remember that summer, and think, *define visit.*

But when people who didn't know the rector heard the complaint, it did a lot of damage.

I recall taking Communion to a dying woman in her home. The paid caregiver watched from the door as I dipped the bread in the wine and laid it gently on the woman's tongue. Then she watched from the sidelines as I visited a few moments with family members who were keeping vigil. The caregiver made one comment toward the end of that time. She said, in a lull in the conversation, "Our minister doesn't visit, you know. This was nice."

It's never the elephant in the room when clergy are discussed critically. Given a chance, it will be named, commented on, commiserated about. I know this. I just wished more people knew what I know about definitions.

Preaching Without Notes

Preaching without notes isn't listed in most descriptions of what a parish is looking for in a new rector. If it was, a whole lot of clergy wouldn't bother applying. A parish will list other attractive qualities it is seeking: outgoing, team player, hard worker, liturgical expert, good preacher, works well with teens and seniors, ecumenically minded. But never this one.

Yet it's a quality that people talk about a lot. When someone has it, it impresses mightily. Someone will be describing a minister they've come across in a mission or another church—seldom in their own—or at a funeral or wedding. "And," they will drop into the conversation in hushed, almost reverential tones, "they preach without notes."

Most of the clergy I've listened to who preached without notes, shouldn't have.

I've timed them. One preached for forty minutes before sitting down. I wasn't sure what her main points were by the end. Call it sour grapes—and you'd probably be right—but I think the best sermons should be focused and limited to less than fifteen minutes. Especially if you have young people listening, whose attention span can be measured in nanoseconds (was that texting I just heard coming from that pew?). Of course, I belong to the Anglican tradition, which in recent centuries hasn't favoured long sermons.

I've also listened to some ministers make up their message on the way to the pulpit or to the middle of the aisle. There was little or no coherent tying of the Scriptures of the day into people's lives, world or local events, or the church's mission.

I've only heard one preacher who could preach well without notes. He didn't really preach, the way most people traditionally think of preaching. He told stories.

His sermons were breath taking, for he'd spin a story within a story within a story, never losing the thread that bound them all together, taking the listener from one reality into another into a landscape that looked vaguely familiar and yet was completely different from the norm.

"Once upon a time," he'd begin, "there was a monk…there was a church…there was a boy…there was a problem."

People would wrap their arms around their legs and stare up at him, mesmerized, as he took them on journeys that were unpredictable and upset long-held assumptions. His stories had twist endings, just like the parables. He could hold your attention well past the longest without-notes preachers I knew.

He was my mentor the first year I was in a parish. He watched my stumbling attempts week in and week out to come up with brilliant sermons (did the people in the pews deserve less?). One day he walked into the vestry and noticed how downcast I was.

"I was up all night wrestling with today's message and it just didn't come together," I told him, feeling desperate and ashamed. What had they hired me for if not, in large part, to give them a weekly message that unpacked the Scriptures and gave light to their week?

"You've got to relax," he counselled. "Not strive for perfection. Just keep it simple. Why don't you try preaching without notes?" he added. "Just to see what it's like." He had noticed the manuscripts typed out in full that I carried into the pulpit.

So the next week I did. Sort of. I had a few notes on a small piece of paper hidden in one palm.

I decided to tell a story, like he might have. And I went from there, only—much to my amazement—referring to my palm once, just to stay on track.

It was exhilarating, scary in the extreme, and freeing.

At the end of my message, I sat down in that space in the service reserved for reflecting on what has just been said. Or for stifled yawning. My mentor stood up, cleared his throat and said, "Now, for those of you who don't already know, this was Bonnie's first sermon preached without notes. How about telling her how you think she did?"

One by one, large white rectangular signs popped up above people's heads: 8.2, 6.6 flipped around quickly to 9.9, 7.5. *Cool!* I thought. *What a people! What a mentor!*

Did I ever do it again? For several months I tried, relying on only a few notes. Gradually I drifted back to full manuscripts.

I tell my students, "If you preach from a full text, make sure you make good eye contact with your congregation. Make sure you're not reading it to them. They need your energy, and you need to see their reaction."

So why, to this day, do I refuse to preach without notes?

For me, part of the process of preparing a message is writing it down and polishing it well. Honing it so it doesn't ramble. Making sure each word is the one best suited to convey the meaning I'm after.

I like the feel of something tangible in front of me, knowing I don't have to worry about blanking at a key moment. My memory isn't as good as it once was, and who has the time to spend going over and over a text in the midst of parish work?

I like where the written word leads as it comes out on the page, detouring and threading back in unexpected ways, revealing more than I knew before starting out ("And my word will not return empty.").

No one will ever say of me, "She preaches without notes." But

I hope someday they will remember that I told stories.

Always Check the Readings of the Day

Most people remember where they were when the planes hit the Twin Towers.

My warden and I were sitting in a greasy spoon several blocks down from the church, drinking copious cups of coffee. His phone buzzed; a moment or two later he looked across at me in a puzzled sort of way and said a plane had just gone into the World Trade Centre. We wrapped up our discussion and for once I headed straight home, turned on the TV and, well, how could you not be horrified and transfixed by the continuous stream of images coming out of New York City?

The footage that paralysed me was of people running down the street between the skyscrapers, a cloud of debris gaining on them like a giant sandstorm. My son had moved to Toronto two weeks before to work at the Eaton Centre, not too far from the CN Tower. Surely it or the tower would be a potential target if Toronto was going to be hit, if this was a deliberate attack on more than the USA. I paced, heart in throat, until he called me on his cell phone and said he wasn't working that day. How far away from downtown was his apartment exactly?

There's another day that doesn't get nearly as much press, but the effects still ripple through the South Shore of Nova Scotia and out into the wider world. If you drive toward Halifax from the tiny fishing village of Blandford, you will find not one, but two memorials, commemorating the crash of Swiss Air Flight 111. Walk around its concrete walls, look at the 229 names, then look out at their burial ground—the camouflaging sea stretching to the horizon. Life was changed forever for far more people than those who died, and their family and friends.

Experts say that when the plane hit the water at more than 340 miles per hour, it was like hitting concrete. Only one "visually identifiable" passenger was recovered. The flight took off from New York City for Geneva, Switzerland on the evening of September 2, 1998. Thirty miles outside Halifax International Airport, after dumping fuel into the waters of St. Margaret's Bay, and with a pilot still trying to put out an on-board fire, it went off the radar.

The first we heard of it was the next morning. My husband turned on the TV for our breakfast news fix, and reports were pouring in of fishermen taking their boats out into the bay to help with rescue and recovery operations, naval ships and helicopters scanning the waters, people huddled on the rocks of Peggy's Cove looking out to sea.

A message to regional clergy came from the bishop's office a day or two later. "If you can give some time to sit with families coming in, please report to the Lord Nelson Hotel." *What could I do?* I thought. Others would be there soon who had better counselling and listening skills than mine. Clergy of all denominations were spreading out to do what they could: clergy at the downtown hotel, clergy receiving families at the airport, clergy sitting with families in tents on the shore of the cove, and in homes opened wide for grieving families.

Sunday was drawing close. What had happened would have to be addressed in prayers and in the sermon. The prayers? Well, that was already well in hand with very capable and sensitive lay people. No need to oversee that; they were better pray-ers than me. But what of the message? The sole responsibility of the message was mine.

What could be said of something too awful for words? What was it that people would be looking for when they came to church in the aftermath? What did they need to hear that would name something they couldn't utter, that would sustain them, perhaps even offer a bit of comfort?

None of them, as far as I knew, were family or friends of the crash victims. How would this impact them beyond the timeframe of the media story? We weren't a church along the coast whose parishioners had welcomed families in from diverse countries, who passed that watery tomb each day on their way to work. We were on the edge of metro, surely no direct impact here.

But there always is, isn't there?

I didn't know then that Leroy had already been called into CFB Shearwater to help with the sorting of recovered items. The gruelling process of confirming who was on the plane was underway so that families would have something to take back with them or hold onto, even if it was only information.

Leroy was an army medic, a slight man in his late thirties, who sat beside his young daughters and wife, three rows down the left-hand side in the church. I didn't know, as I looked at my blank page, that he was handling materials each day, and would be for months to come, that would sear into his heart and soul.

"Make sure you always check the readings of the day," a wise mentor once told me in my student minister days. "Even if it's a special occasion, and you already have your subject matter identified, check the set readings. You'll be surprised by what you'll find there."

Her words came to mind as I stared at my blank screen. So I checked. Gospel reading: nothing relevant to this situation there. Epistle: nothing there either. Old Testament reading: zip.

What about the psalm for Sunday? *Yeah, but no one ever preaches on the psalms,* my inner editor said.

The Book of Psalms is placed strategically in the centre of the Bible, so the pages naturally fall open there. The Book of Psalms, an ancient hymnal of a God-fearing, stiff-necked people; their poetic responses to often hideous circumstances. The one book of the Bible that is purely a one-sided conversation: *Here's how I feel, Lord… Here's what I'm handling; fix it! Kill my enemies, vindicate me… Save the people, Lord… I'm sorry; please make me clean inside… Explain your silence, Lord, don't abandon me. I'm in despair.* The Book of Psalms: my favourite reading material because I like its rawness and truth.

I turned to the psalm appointed for Sunday. And there it was, the words illuminated as though in gold. Not an answer to why this had happened. No word of deliverance. No promise of protection from hurt for those who remained.

Where was God when this happened? That was the real question some of us had that morning, as we woke to a world so different from the day before.

In those final fear-filled moments, in the silence of the watery descent and twisted steel, in the molecules of humanity spread out too far to ever reassemble, God was present. An anonymous poet affirmed this thousands of years ago in these poignantly relevant words:

"If I take the wings of the morning and dwell in the uttermost parts of the sea, even there your hand will lead me and your right hand hold me fast." *Psalm 139*

The Vows We Make

Clergy handle the extremes, sometimes on the same day.

In the morning, you sit beside an old man as he gently holds his wife's hand, kisses her goodbye, and watches as the machine that keeps her alive is disconnected. The heartbeats stretch out on the monitor until there is only a straight line. They haven't been apart for any length of time in sixty years. You look back as you leave the hospital room and see him sitting there alone.

That afternoon you wind your stole around the hands of two young people whom you have just pronounced married. You say a blessing over them and send them off down the aisle and out into the rest of their lives to resounding applause from family and friends. What lies ahead of them, you wonder, and do they have any understanding at all what living out the vows they've just made may someday require?

I'm one of those clergy who would rather "do" ten funerals than one wedding. According to the Gospel of John, one of the first things Jesus did after he began full-time ministry was attend a wedding. But he was a guest, not the presiding rabbi. He didn't have to deal with overbearing parents or brides, with fainting grooms, with requests for unity candle or sand pouring micro services, with country and western music played during the signing of the register, or photographers who don't listen.

"Why do you want to get married in the church?" is one of my favourite questions to couples I don't know who want me to marry them.

I asked it at a premarital workshop one year as I looked out over fifteen couples who had assembled in the church hall. All the couples that day were in their twenties and early thirties. Most looked back at me with blank faces.

"Well, it's our family church," one person ventured. "My parents would be disappointed if we weren't married there." *Pressure by parents.*

"We were driving by and we stopped in. It's a beautiful place for a wedding," another added. *Photo op.*

"It's more personal than a wedding chapel or a Justice of the Peace ceremony," someone said.

Now that takes me back.

I was sitting in the parish office one day when the phone rang. It was a woman who sounded rather impatient.

"Do you do weddings at your church?" she asked.

"Yes," I said, wishing already that we didn't.

"Well, good. And who do I have to talk to about booking one?"

"That would be me *(unfortunately),*" I said.

"Well…here's what I want."

Not getting off to a good start, I thought. "Maybe you should come in to see me, to discuss this in person."

"Nope, I want to do this quickly and the phone's just fine. I don't want anything spiritual in the wedding."

"Excuse me?"

"Nothing about God or Jesus or anything like that. Just something straightforward and quick."

"Well," I squeaked out, trying to recover, "why do you want to be married in a church then?"

"It's cheaper than the wedding chapel or a Justice of the Peace," she explained impatiently.

"How much do they charge?"

"Two hundred dollars! Can you believe it?" she huffed.

"But you haven't asked me what the church charges," I said. Silence.

"We charge a thousand dollars for the basic package plus something for the altar guild and the…"

Slam went the receiver. Treat us like a service industry, and, well, it was the best wedding I never did.

Only one couple at the workshop got anywhere close to what I was hoping to hear. "Well, the church is part of our lives and we can't imagine saying our vows anywhere else." Wow! They were from my parish, by the way.

Strip all the fuss and decorations away, and a wedding is about a couple making public what they decided privately some time before—to be faithful to each other. They don't need to do that in a church, with a priest.

On my more cynical days, I think all clergy should be freed from the obligation to perform marriages. Let couples get hitched in a civil ceremony. Get all the documentation taken care of; be married in the province's eyes. Then, and only then, ask for the church's blessing. Or God's, pronounced by a minister.

I suspect only a few couples would do that. Those who have roots in the church already.

Why so jaded? Any number of reasons.

In one of the closing prayers in the "new" prayer book, the service says, "Let them be an example to their community." "But why can't you say we were living separately before the wedding?" the young man asked me. "This is going to affect our social assistance."

Pause. "You are asking me, a minister…" (*got to underscore that fact right now*) "to lie?" I asked.

"Well…yes."

Paying the organist was the one fee the church required. There was no charge for the use of the church, or for the minister's services. "Sure I'll pay the organist," said the offended groom. "I said I would, and I will make sure a cheque is dropped off." It never was. I paid the organist.

"You look at me differently now," he said months later. "When I see you at funerals I remember my promise that we'd start coming to church if you married us. I intend to keep my word." *About the cheque too?* I wondered.

Then there's the wedding rehearsal, which can break the most seasoned clergy. There's the scenario you hope for in the best of all circumstances, and then there's the one that so often unfolds.

Hoped for: Family and all other participants arrive on time.

More likely to happen: Participants straggle in. Some key ones don't arrive for quite a while, others can't make it.

Can happen: Rehearsal is at a church not your own. Everyone is late, by about an hour. Choir is waiting in nearby hall to practice in church. No one's told you that. You are blasted for being late wrapping up rehearsal.

Hoped for: Minister explains some key guidelines to a church wedding including not taking photos except during certain times, throwing of confetti (don't do it!). Everyone nods in agreement.

Can happen: Minister begins to explain guidelines concerning photo taking during service, throwing of confetti…. Father of Bride jumps up, asks, "Where the hell did those rules come from?" Bride and mother cringe. He doesn't remember the church having rules like that when he used to attend.

Hoped for: Prior to rehearsal, the couple has talked at least once with organist/musician about the music they like and that's appropriate (guidelines provided by minister). On the night of rehearsal, the music person is at keyboard/guitar/other instrument ready for cue.

Can happen: Couple has decided against a live musician, has chosen music on a CD. Hasn't chosen anyone to cue music at rehearsal or wedding. Expects the church to have a sound system they can use. It doesn't. Music is not what would normally be played in a church (read: understatement).

Hoped for: Rehearsal begins. Everyone pays close attention. Wedding parties line up at front (groom and his party) and at door (bride, attendants, father or other person giving her away), ready for instruction.

More likely to happen: Small kids run around church, jump up and down on steps behind minister. Conversations continue in the pews. Some attendants begin decorating ends of pews.

Hoped for: The dry run is a huge success. Everyone knows when music is to begin, how to walk down the aisle properly, where they are to stand, when to come forward for readings, to hold flowers, to witness papers, to exchange rings. Groom and bride and all parents are visibly more relaxed. Practice wraps up in less than an hour. Church is locked up and minister heads home.

More likely to happen: Practice is absolute chaos. The flower girl doesn't want to walk down the aisle first. The ring bearer wants to walk only beside his mom. Groomsmen cannot figure out how to maintain a straight line near the groom. Bridesmaids sprint up the aisle despite instructions. The microphone isn't working. Readers haven't practiced their passages yet. No one can find the wedding pillows the bride and groom are to kneel on during the prayers. A parent asks just when the unity candle/sand is supposed to be lit/poured. (Oops, forgot to include that.) The minister says, "It may look like a smozzle now, but it will be just fine tomorrow." The family finishes decorating the church after the practice. The minister sticks around to lock up the church and misses own date night with spouse.

All of which is why I really don't enjoy rehearsals, necessary though they are.

Most weddings, on the other hand, have their own peculiar beauty. They usually start on time; a good thing for the groom who is sitting beside his best man in a small vestry room trying to focus.

Most people are more than willing to abide by a few guidelines, though I do remember a professional photographer leaping over an altar rail to get in front of a recessing couple. And bottles of bubbles—not bubbly—have largely replaced confetti.

Startling things happen at weddings.

The got-everything-under-control bride of the rehearsal night can't keep her legs from shaking as she heads down the aisle. She and her groom make their vows sitting down in chairs facing each other.

The painfully shy groom practices his vows for weeks beforehand so that he can say them without prompting. As he starts to say, "I, Bob, take you, Katherine, to be my wedded husband," laughter breaks out. The minister glares at everyone snickering, silence descends and the groom begins again.

The groom begins to cry halfway through his promises. The bride laughs nervously. The minister produces Kleenex. Everyone takes a deep breath, refocuses.

The bride catches the heel of her shoe on her long train as she and her new husband start down the sanctuary stairs at the end of the service. She pitches forward; he catches her. Someday she will say that's what he's done all their married lives.

The little ring bearer lifts up his pillow, expecting the little plastic ring to be blessed just like the other rings were.

In the end it doesn't matter if the choreography is slightly off, the pillows don't appear, the lines are askew, someone forgot to unbox a ring before that part of the service is reached. It doesn't matter that the flower girl keeps picking up the petals she threw down a moment before, or that the ring bearer carried the pillow upside down (unless it's the real ring), or that a bridesmaid got her high heel stuck in the grate that lay in wait in the centre of the aisle. This is the stuff of family myth. And a perfect wedding would be a boring wedding.

No one usually remembers what advice the minister tried to dispense just before the vows. They only remember the couple, young or old, first time-rounders or marriage veterans, who stood in front of everyone and said, "I will love and comfort and protect you, forsaking all others, through all circumstances/with my body I thee honour, in sickness and in health, for richer and for poorer, for as long as we both shall live."

Look closely and you will see old married couples reaching out to touch hands, soon-to-be spouses taking notes, emotional parents startled by the mature young couple standing in front of the minister, the slightly less cynical look on the face of a survivor of divorce.

The Great Adventure lies ahead.

It will lead through tangled, dark valleys they cannot imagine and for which they are unprepared. Along the way, each will be changed. They will disappoint and be disappointed. Wound and be wounded. They will know moments shot through with joy, and also know dread. They will have opportunities to learn more about themselves: how far they can stretch without breaking, what happens when they do break, what happens if they don't even try.

They may find the way too hard and decide to give up. They may continue to journey together as bitter and twisted versions of their former selves. Or they may persevere, with God's help—I like adding that bit—each one carrying the other part of the way. It's an adventure after all, not a walk in the park.

If they are blessed and especially strong of heart, they will love much and deeply. Perhaps someday they may even find themselves in a hospital room holding a wrinkled-but-familiar hand, or having it held as this journey slips away.

For now though, as they set off down the aisle and into the celebrations, anything's possible.

But Will the Gown Still Fit? And Some Baptisms to Remember

Timing is everything, especially when it comes to baptism.

The bishop's guidelines were clear. "Baptism is an important rite not to be undertaken lightly or without proper preparation. Try to establish set dates in your parish, such as All Saints Day, Baptism of the Lord, Easter, Pentecost, Transfiguration.... Baptisms should not happen on demand." Translation: not whenever people want them.

Every Anglican rector has to figure out how to handle baptisms.

First, there's the initial contact—a phone call or someone at the door of the church, who asks about getting a baby "done." These are disguised pressure situations that can lead to hasty, ill-thought-out responses. Far better to book a time to go to see them in person, I've learned. I might have avoided the following responses circulating through the community:

"The minister said I had to jump through all sorts of hoops before my baby could be baptized." Preparation is indeed required. Certainly not as much as for adult baptism, but some, which parents and godparents (sponsors) are expected to attend. No hoops involved.

"The minister said, 'No, not unless you come to church first.'" That's how my invitation to come back to church was interpreted?

"The minister refused to even discuss it with me," said the grandma. I asked her to get the parents to contact me.

"Well," said another clearly exasperated grandma, "things have certainly changed since I went to church." And that, dear lady, is why they have changed. Once upon a time most people went to church and understood their faith; nowadays most people don't. There has to be some teaching.

Then there is the first sit-down to discuss what the church considers baptism to be, and whether or not this is the time for getting their baby "done." If the gown is going to be an issue, it will be raised here. Perhaps in a conversation like this:

"But I thought we could set the baptismal date for next week."

"What's the rush?"

"Or sometime really soon."

Silence as the minister waits for first mention of…

"Well, there's this gown, you see, that's been in the family for years. The baby's growing fast and soon it will be too small."

Over the years I have moved from a barely concealed curled lip—you've got to be kidding…fix a date around that!—to a more appreciative response.

"It would mean the world to us if you could do this." That plea is usually the final sally, accompanied by a beseeching look.

Nowhere do the bishop's guidelines mention the gown.

Nor do the instructions that preface the service in any prayer book. There are lengthy descriptions of other powerful symbols in the service. There's water, to make clean, to recall the waters of creation and the Jordan in which Jesus was baptized, and the waters of birth. Light, in the form of a candle lit from the big Pascal or Christ candle, and passed on to this brand new person, a little light in the world representing the Light of the World. And holy oil (chrism), which some priests use to make a cross on the forehead of the newly baptized, oil to recall anointing of royalty and priests in Old Testament times, hard-to-remove oil to represent being marked as Christ's own forever.

There is no mention of the gown. Yet people aren't just trying to be difficult when they insist on its presence. Something else is in play here.

Some baptismal gowns are passed down through families. They are handed down through the generations from parent to child, or from sibling to sibling, cousin to cousin. With each wearing, the gown gains significance and more stories attach to the tradition. "My great-grandmother made this gown out of flour bags, and then embroidered it."

"My aunt made this for me when I first became pregnant. She died a few months ago."

"This was mine. Mom kept it for me all these years. Here's a photo of that Easter Sunday; that's me in my dad's arms."

What is happening in these moments?

Is it a recalling of the past in such a way that it is present again? The church has a name for this: anamnesis. Maybe it's a way of connecting to ancestors, and a desire to include this child in the story of all the family faithful who have gone before.

Whatever it is, it is powerful.

On the day my son was baptized, he actually fit into the gown I had worn at my own christening. It had ruffles and lace and little puffy sleeves. It was much too feminine for someone who, even as a baby, looked all boy. Any photos taken that day were fortunately from a distance. We made it through the service, my mom beaming at her first grandchild and fingering the gown absentmindedly, perhaps remembering a baptism long before. I didn't ask.

The reception that followed was packed with family and

friends. My son wore a far more comfortable, manly sleeper. The baptismal gown was soaking in the bathroom sink: he had pooped all over it on the drive home. A comment, perhaps, on how some things should not be passed on.

Another baptism. The required preparation had been done, the date set, and now it was here. It was one of the bishop's suggested days for baptism, All Saints Day. The church was filled to capacity; not hard to do when the church holds less than a hundred people and it's a baptism. The child's extended family turned out in full force—grandparents, uncles and aunts, cousins.

At each meeting prior to the baptism, the mom mentioned how important the gown was. She didn't say why. She ended up putting a gusset in the gown so it would still fit her son on his big day.

At the end of the service, she stood up to introduce her family. Each of these people, she said, had worn this gown sometime during the last seventy years. Fifteen people stood up. There were seniors, people in their forties and thirties including the mom, and twenties, several teens, the baby's toddler sister.

Question: Why is a baptismal gown sometimes like a church pew?

Answer: In the eyes of some, both are holy.

* * *

A few baptisms stand out in memory, though any time I've held a child in my arms at the font, or stood there beside adult candidates and made the sign of the cross on their forehead; when I've said those words that have been spoken down through the ages, "I mark you as Christ's own forever," I have had a tough time holding back tears.

George

George was a toddler. His parents decided it was time now for them to return to church and get him started on his Christian journey. George was very active and this concerned his parents. "You won't be able to hold him yourself when you baptize him," the mom said. "He may not react well to the water."

But I was an old hand at baptisms, having at least a dozen to my credit. The day before his baptism, we stood around the solid stone font, looking down at the water I had just poured. His mom and his dad and his grandparents and godparents watched as I held him up and let him splash the waters. "See," I said, "it's warm. And tomorrow I am going to pour some water over your head just like this." His blue eyes registered surprise at the trickles now running down his face. I mopped them up gently with the baptismal towel, and handed him back to his dad. "That wasn't so bad," I said.

George was dressed in a white suit complete with a silver vest. He made quite a picture that morning. Thus far in the service, he had played quietly in the front pew. Maybe this wasn't one of his especially active days, I thought. It was time to proceed to the font. We moved down through the full congregation who turned to watch. Cameras were surreptitiously being removed from purses and jackets everywhere.

George's dad was standing next to me at the font, holding onto him firmly. I splashed the warm waters like I had the day before. "Would you like to splash, too?" I asked. He shook his head. His dad lowered him down to my level and closer to the waters of the font. Blue eyes stared at me as I scooped up a shell full of water. Then, too fast to register, his hand came up, full force, and struck me on the cheek. *Thwack*!

The congregation gasped. His mom looked appalled. His dad kept holding on.

George was baptized that morning. His dad poured the water over him and gently mopped up the trickles running down his face. I said the words. Brought me to tears.

Sunrise Service

Six a.m. is early for most people to rise. Six a.m. is far too early for most to be standing out in the dark around a just-lit fire. Those who brave the hour and the cold are rewarded with a glorious service that is multi-faceted and rich in symbolism: Sunrise service on Easter morning.

It begins with the lighting of the new fire and the Pascal candle under a night sky, sometimes with snowflakes drifting down, and all the people huddled close. That's followed by the procession into the darkened church, standing with tapers lit from the Pascal candle as one voice sings an ancient hymn about Christ's resurrection. Lights come on and the church is revealed in trumpet-shaped flowers and white and gold hangings. The salvation story is told in passages from Genesis, Exodus, Isaiah, Psalms, Romans, and the Gospels.

The table is spread with homemade bread and rich wine, and then offered at the rail. Taste and see—and hear and feel and smell—that the Lord is good!

Sometimes there is baptism too.

Her name was Rhea. She was in her mid-twenties and preparing to marry in a few months. Another clergy recommended that she and her fiancé, John, check out our church. They came one week and liked the atmosphere and the music. They kept coming. It became their spiritual home.

In the course of marriage preparation, Rhea asked about being baptized. She wanted to explore her spirituality further. She and John joined an Alpha course, and we set her baptism for Easter Sunday at the sunrise service.

Rhea and John stood beside their parents and friends, taking everything in. I asked the age-old questions of "Do you renounce…Do you turn to… Do you put your whole trust in… Do you promise to…" and she answered in a clear voice, heavy with emotion. I poured the water over her and traced the cross in oil on her forehead. She took her place at the rail beside her fiancé, and held up her hands to receive the bread and the wine for the first time.

The Baptists call it a "Believer's Baptism." No worrying here that parents and sponsors would forget their promises to raise her in the knowledge and love of Christ. She'd chosen for herself.

She smiled shyly at me as I placed the bread in her hands and said, "The body of Christ given for you." It's Easter morning, first light. The Son has risen.

Grandson

How must that be, I thought, watching my colleague, *to say words over your own grandson that you have said over so many others? To dip your thumb in the oil and make the sign that you live your life by on his little forehead? Pass the little candle to his parents as you say, as though you were saying it to him, "Receive the light of Christ to show that you have passed from darkness to light." And join with the responding congregation, "Let your light so shine before others…" wondering perhaps how he will shine in the years to come, knowing you will do your best by him always. How must that be?*

I didn't expect to get the chance. My kids and grandson lived in another part of the country and seldom came to visit. My husband and I had gotten used to the idea that our grandson would grow up without us being an important part of his life. *Skype can only go so far*, I remember thinking cynically.

Then the improbable happened. They all moved home,

within driving distance. And everything changed.

We set the baptism date for the Day of the Lord's Baptism in early January. The kids chose the smallest church in the parish, the one in which they felt most comfortable for the service. Invitations went out to our closest friends.

And yes, the parents had to go through preparation just like everyone else. No exceptions, especially for family. That was the rule. My rule, anyway.

I made my own usual preparations for a baptism. I got the information for the certificate and filled out the documents. *How peculiar*, I thought, *to be writing such a familiar name in the baptismal register.* I set up the font; the towel draped over one edge, with oil and Pascal candle and little baptismal candle to one side. I asked someone to bring warm water the next morning; there was no running water in this church, and I worried I might just forget it in all the excitement at the rectory.

The church was filling up and the kids were early for once. They took their place near the front, holding our grandson. He wore a tiny white suit; no puffy sleeves for him.

Two generations of friends and sponsors (godparents) crammed into the front two pews, and memories crammed in with them. I remembered my good friend Nadine, standing beside me the day our son left home at nineteen for work in another province; planning an 86th birthday reception for my mother-in-law that last year she lived with us; making sure both of her sons made it to Toronto for our son's wedding. I remembered her husband, Stephen, walking with us on salt marsh trails early mornings; standing in the middle of the street with our dog, now his, as my husband and I said goodbye and headed off to another city. We'd been through a lot together.

Their sons sat behind them, trying to get comfortable in the old pew. They were friends of our son, both of whom, like him, had headed out of province for work and then had come back again. One was sitting with his wife. I remembered the couple standing in front of me, exchanging rings and vows, and looking impossibly grown up.

I shouldn't have looked up. Too many memories were flooding into too full a heart. It was all leaking out. I tried to catch my husband's eye, but he was overflowing too.

The music began, and it was a hymn we all knew. My priestly colleague stood at the front, playing a special song on his guitar. It was the same one he'd played at his own grandson's baptism.

Every time I looked up, I saw more. The light streamed in through the plain glass windows. There wasn't a space to spare in any pew. Faces I hadn't known two years before when I first came to the parish, smiled up at me. Some winked. There were our friends—most of the ones we had in the world—and our faith family, too.

And what do I do if I can't get this lump out of my throat?

I picked up our grandson, held him close, rocking slowly side to side. *And you doubted you would ever have this moment?*

I leaned into the beautifully carved wooden font, cupped the warm water in one hand, and poured it over him. "I baptize you in the name of the Father, and of the Son, and of the Holy Spirit."

The light shining in, the warmth of memories, the music lifting us up, new friends and old gathered together like threads in a luminous tapestry, the old words becoming new again, the baby bound forever to my heart, the water pouring down: all of it was pure grace.

It's Not Just Fundraising

"What do you think of fundraising in a parish?"

The question was asked during my initial interview. Even then, I knew there was no simple answer.

I looked around the table at the members of the selection committee for any hint of their opinions. Nada. *Best be honest—always a good attribute for a minister to demonstrate,* I thought.

"Well, in the best of all worlds there would be no need for it. People would be tithing and there would be lots of money for bills and maintenance, outreach, and new ministries." A few heads nodded in agreement.

"But tithing isn't practiced widely in most parishes, and so there is usually a need for fundraisers. And, of course, there are other benefits fundraising brings with it." I had the attention of the others now. Since then, I have found that raising money is the least of all the benefits.

The Launch

Putting together a parish cookbook can be a dicey, political undertaking. Dicey because having one person responsible for typing or assembly can bring everything to a crashing halt if they bail or, worse, say they just don't have time to do it now but will soon. On the political side, just how do you decide which biscuit recipe to include out of fifteen submissions?

Neither of these considerations fazed the committee of four. "Why not do a cookbook?" they said. "It'll be a perfect way to showcase some of the culinary talents in all four churches, and have our own anniversary project."

So the call went out for local recipes that had been handed down through the generations. The ad in the parish bulletin said, "Please include a tiny story about why this recipe is special to you, where it came from, and any memories attached to it."

The project ticked along like clockwork. Recipes came in by the bunches: handwritten, typed, and e-mailed. The youngest member of the committee, April, compiled them as they came in. Bids were invited and a local printer won, who began working with the committee to decide on cover art, how the pages would look, and any photos to include.

The committee agreed a book launch would be the perfect method to raise interest and promote sales. The day of the launch came on a crisp, clear November afternoon.

The low-ceilinged church basement had been transformed. Small circular tables for four were set up in the centre of the room, each draped in white linen and decked out with fresh flowers and china teacups. Hot food stations, featuring dishes from the book, stretched the length of two intersecting walls. Behind each station stood that dish's creator, wearing a tall chef's hat and sporting a name tag that said the name of the dish and the page number from the book. Hot coleslaw, hash brown casserole, tenderloin tips, baked spaghetti and other dishes were on offer. A table with various breads, biscuits, and desserts stood along a third wall, featuring gingerbread, pineapple muffins, pound cake, cookies, puddings, and pies. The woman at one end of it pointed out her World War II cookies, explaining how they were made from basic rations.

The parish band took their places on the platform set up along the fourth wall. On an adjacent table, between bouquets of flowers, cookbooks were laid out for perusing.

April sat at the table just inside the door, boxes of recipe books stacked up around her, ready to fill orders. Each book was $10. The cost of printing had been less than half that. "We got a discount by assembling them ourselves," she told me.

"So," I asked her, as I picked up a few books for gifts, "how many did we print in all?" She named a number that nearly made me choke.

I have always encouraged committees to think big. "If you're going to do something, do it well," I've said. Someone was clearly listening. *How on Earth will we sell enough to pay for the print run, let alone make any money?* Of course, that wasn't the main reason for doing the project, but still....

The doors opened and the first ones in were the seniors, mostly women. They sat down at the tables and didn't leave. They drank their tea and coffee, obviously enjoying the fine china and the samples from all around the room. The band played quietly and well, setting the tone, not at all put off at the laughter and the rising voices all around them.

People drifted up to the stations, asked questions, and identified which recipes they were sampling in the book. Chefs talked with other chefs, exchanging stories about their dishes.

One of the oldest women in the parish stood and recited a poem, which everyone could hear because of the hush that descended at her first words. A friend at the same table sat looking up at her, eyes shining. They had been friends for close to eighty years.

The band played on. The reporter for the local newspaper held her plate of samples in one hand, grinning, and took some pictures of the committee and the printer. April was barely keeping up with the demand for books. Servers wandered through with plates of hors d'oeuvres. No one was giving up their chairs at the little tables.

They covered the cost of the printing at the launch. *Oh ye of little faith!* There was no charge for coming in and sampling—only the request that you consider buying a book.

Flowers for Cancer

My grandma on my dad's side could grow anything anywhere. Just give her some rich black muck and some barnyard fertilizer and let her loose. Produce spilled over from her small garden patch, raspberry canes bent under the weight of their fruit, and strawberries grew the size of tablespoons. Her flower gardens were the stuff of gardeners' dreams, ribbons of colour at least two feet deep, weaving through the white picket fence about her front yard.

Me? My husband would see my eyes light up each spring as we drove by the local greenhouse, and say, "Do the plants a favour. Leave them there."

So it was with some trepidation that I was listening to the suggestion being made by our parish administrator in her office one September morning. It was her response to a challenge recently issued to all the congregations in the parish to come up with some unique proposals for outreach in our communities. What she was proposing was a Garden of Hope for the rectory's front yard. A good location, she pointed out, because the rectory sat in the middle of the parish, highly visible to anyone driving through our communities.

"We could sell daffodil bulbs in memory of those who had died from cancer, and in celebration of people currently fighting cancer and of those who have beaten it so far. We can order the bulbs in bulk," my administrator continued. "Maybe council would agree to donate the monies to buy them. We could invite a representative from the Canadian Cancer Society to come on the day we plant them and officially receive a cheque from the parish.

We could actually raise a fair amount, I suspect," she finished.

Wow! I thought. *Someone actually took up the challenge!* It had a great focus. As in all communities, few families in our parish had escaped being touched by cancer. I had buried more parishioners than I cared to remember because of it. No age group was immune, and many family schedules revolved around chemo and radiation treatments in the city. Her suggestion was brilliant. *Will the flowers survive my care, though?*

On a cold, mid-November afternoon, we gathered around a freshly-created flower bed set perpendicular between the front of the rectory and the highway. Eighteen holes pockmarked the soil, waiting for bulbs. Over two hundred bulbs had been sold.

Snowflakes drifted down as names (in memory of…in celebration for…) were read from a parchment-type scroll. The thirty-five or so people who stood huddled together around the bed held their bulbs close for the reading of the names and the prayers that followed.

We prayed for courage and for letting go; we prayed for new advances in research; we gave thanks for blessings in the midst of illness. We presented a cheque for a thousand dollars to the local cancer society representative. One by one, people knelt down on the cold soil, placed their bulbs in the holes, and covered them up gently.

Sometime that winter, a tole painting artist in the parish offered to create a sign for the garden. It said "Garden of Hope" in white letters woven around daffodils on a black background. It was perfect for the top of the garden and would be clearly visible to all passers-by.

That first spring I waited and waited for the first shoots to break through. Each day I checked for evidence of their survival. Daffodils eventually appeared in abundance and in such different colours: yellow on yellow, yellow with orange centres, cream with yellow, cream with orange.

Not long after her gift of the sign, the artist died suddenly. Of cancer.

ATV Run

"But no one will come if alcohol's not allowed," a council member said. The ATVers among us all nodded.

All except me. "Let's just try it," I said. "What can it hurt? We might even set a precedent."

We were already breaking new ground if we went ahead with our plans for an ATV run. We'd been tossing around ideas for a unique fundraiser for some time now; one that would appeal to the larger community, would be fun, and not a whole lot of work. Tough criteria. But this idea seemed to meet them all.

Council passed the idea, though not without some reservations.

Once the planning got underway, however, attitudes shifted. Frank offered his camp as a meeting place after the run. "We'll set up for something hot to eat and drink," he said. "Everybody will be cold by then." A council member, Dan, who was also a veteran of ATV runs, said he'd plot out a course, make sure it was interesting and long enough, and had options that would appeal to those who liked slower-paced runs and those who wanted to hot-foot it. Everyone agreed it sounded great. We just had to set a date and get the word out in the larger community. Having members of local ATV clubs on council didn't hurt with the publicity.

They set the run for just after hunting season. The consensus was that it was safer that way. It would cover a lot of territory along the old logging roads that crisscrossed the backcountry. "Even seasoned ATVers haven't explored all of them," Dan said, "so it's sure to surprise."

The night he announced the route, people at the table stared off into space, no doubt imagining coming across a bull moose or a bear around some bend. Most had done so at least once or twice, and a whole lot closer to home than this run would end up taking them. Some told tales of timber wolves that weren't that far-fetched, considering how close we were to the Maine border and how thick the woods were. The run would be six hours long, starting at 10 a.m. at the church, Dan added, and he would do a dry run a few days before just to make sure the roads were safe.

The day before the run, a torrential rain began late in the afternoon and went on through the night.

Twenty-four ATVs showed up at the church the next morning. A few had passengers. More than half were people I had never seen before.

One dad, with his ten-year-old son on the back of his vehicle, approached the organizers.

"Thanks for having a run without alcohol," he said. "None of the other organized runs excluded it. I can bring my son along on this one."

I tried not to look smug.

Everyone was bundled up against the cold so only a small part of their faces showed. It was hard to recognize anyone from any direction, I thought, as I climbed up behind my husband on our oversized bike. The roar of engines drowned out last-minute instructions. One by one, we all pulled out onto the trail.

At the two-hour mark, we broke for a few minutes, pulling the rigs into a circle on a stretch of rocky cliff overlooking a valley. The coffee tasted pretty good straight out of a thermos cup. Its warmth soaked into my icy mittens. Sandwiches were pulled from back packs and wolfed down. Dan set up a little gas stove on the front of his machine and cooked up some hot dogs for anyone interested. *Such a view from this spot*, I thought. *It does the heart good.* People stood around sipping their coffees, shifting from one cold foot to the other, just looking and looking.

The cliff was the departure point for the separate routes; one group headed off on the fast route which was longer. The rest of us stayed on the turtle route. The hope was that everyone would end up at the camp around the same time.

Several miles farther along, a stretch of twenty or so feet of no-road lay before the bikes. Big boulders stuck out of a stream that was still gushing debris where the road had once been. The water was moving fast. We could either go through it or go home.

Dan was visibly upset. I could see him worrying clear across the cluster of bikes. *What if someone gets hurt here? Will the church insurance cover them? This is the last time I ever leave a route unchecked after a storm.* Then, very carefully, one of the men lowered one wheel down into the surging water, one wheel up slightly on the edge of a boulder. He gingerly made his way down into the washout, inch by inch. The bike kept going. Up and down large rocks, across some flat ones, through the swift-moving water, the ATV pressed on until it finally was up the far bank and onto road again. The less-experienced bikers followed him one by one, while others shouted instructions from the sides, ready to pitch in and winch anyone out if need be. Passengers who had driven with them climbed up on the bigger bikes with the most seasoned drivers, and made their way across.

"I thought we were done there," Dan said later, shivering. "Nothing prepared me for that. It could have gone wrong."

Wow! I thought, standing on the far side. *Now that's ATVing!*

The turtles beat the hot-footers back to camp by about half an hour. "Showed them," one of the senior ATVers said. By the time people pulled into camp, they were cold to the bone, despite layers of clothing and extra mitts.

Frank's camp was set on the bend of a river. The water glittered bronze in the late afternoon sun. Old pines edged the property, offering protection from the wind.

A large, well-tended bonfire blazed close to the river and

a few people were seated there already. Someone got up and occasionally poked at the fire.

Long, narrow tables from the church were set up in front of the camp building. They groaned under big urns of coffee and tea, pots of home-baked beans, bacon on a griddle, slices of ham, pickles, and thickly-sliced, homemade brown bread. *This is heavenly,* I sighed, as I put a spoonful of steaming beans into my mouth.

The main course was so well received—most everyone had seconds—that no one had room for dessert. A whole table of pies and cakes and squares and cookies just sat there, untouched. My husband, who had a sweet tooth, looked like he might cry.

Frank said, "Well, let's just auction them off, then."

They made more money on the desserts than they did on the run. No one went home disappointed. Some were already planning a sequel.

Define Success

A new group was in charge of the Pancake Supper. After almost thirty years of very successful Shrove Tuesday suppers, the former leaders had passed on the pancake mix.

In the kitchen all was in readiness: hams were sliced and heating up in the oven, sausages were being turned, someone brought a long, deep container of orange slices over for garnish, stacks of takeout containers sat beside stacks of plates, mix was poured onto hot griddles and watched for bubbles then flipped, blueberry and strawberry sauce was set aside for special requests near the pass-thru.

In the dining area, jugs of maple syrup and plates of butter sat out on the white paper-covered tables. Places were set for the first run of hungry customers. The dessert table overflowed with different toppings for ice cream—cherries, Smarties, coconut, chocolate sprinkles, and caramel and chocolate sauces—and with apple crisp and a fluffy diabetic pineapple dish for those who didn't want ice cream. Two women everyone trusted hovered behind it, flexing their hands in anticipation of scooping and slicing. The ticket taker, seated just inside the door, was ready.

But a major snowstorm forecast days ago had materialized. The kitchen crew had waded through drifts to get here several hours ago. Would anyone turn up for the supper in this mess? The hour for the supper to begin was at hand. "Let's just see what happens," we all agreed.

The winds hit the door like a hammer, and a few people were buffeted in. It wasn't the usual line waiting out the door on a Shrove Tuesday, for sure. "Might not be a second sitting," someone said. "Might barely fill this one," another amended.

The phone in the kitchen rang. It kept ringing. Takeout orders were coming in, a lot more than anticipated. Three of the extra hands in the kitchen volunteered to help deliver the orders. Neighbours and spouses were arriving now sporadically to pick up orders and have supper before they headed out again. "Keep this warm, would you?"

A vanload from a neighbouring parish unloaded at the side door, and bundled up people made their way carefully down the steps. "We've not missed a pancake supper here in over ten years, and no storm was going to stop us tonight," the driver said, as he unwrapped his scarf and took off his hat. Someone pulled out a mop to keep the melting snow from making the floor too slippery.

The smell of pancakes and sausages filled the air. The special blueberry and strawberry sauces seemed to go a lot further; almost everyone who braved the wild winds and snowdrifts got to sample some. The normal, frantic pace was slower in the kitchen and around the tables. There was more time for one-on-one conversations with customers.

The blizzard raged on. Occasionally, if we listened closely, we could hear one of the mega snow plows go by. Inside the church hall, all was calm and running smoothly. With the extra take-outs, we would at least cover our costs. A couple of servers said they'd drop off some of the leftover dinners to people at a local seniors' complex on their way home. "They'll appreciate something special like this," one said. Another agreed the price was right.

We barely had enough people show up for one sitting, even when we included ourselves, but that was okay. We'd kept a tradition going; people who counted on the supper hadn't been disappointed. All of us—workers from the kitchen and dining room—sat down together and poured maple syrup over our suppers.

"Heard they almost didn't make ends meet," one of the former leaders said the next day at the Ash Wednesday service. "Hardly a success," she added.

"Define success," I said.

Lighting the Night

We were sitting in our newly renovated church, me and eight other members of church council. Everyone had turned out to do a bit of planning for the next few months, before the frenzied pace of Christmas took over.

"We've probably missed Christmas," the elegant, grey-haired senior announced.

I focused on her a bit better than I had been. *So many distractions this time of year,* I was thinking. *What is she on about? Christmas is still four weeks away.*

"Remember the bulbs we sold for the Garden of Hope? Everyone appreciated that idea and the service that was held. There was great support for it all across our communities. Well,

I've been thinking of another kind of bulb."

Figuratively speaking, my own light bulb was switching on. I'd just been to the local firefighter's annual tree lighting ceremony a few evenings before.

"What if we had our own tree this year? And we sold bulbs in memory of people and then after a little service in the church, we went outside and switched on all the lights? What do you think? Would it work? The firefighters wouldn't get annoyed, would they?" she asked.

"It has merit," someone said.

"I like it," added the warden.

"But it's a bit late, don't you think, to be selling bulbs and getting anything together before Christmas?" the secretary asked.

"What if," someone suggested, "we had an Epiphany tree?"

Everyone sat back for a moment, considering. Epiphany, the season right after Christmas. At Epiphany, the Christmas tree that we put up on the vacant lot next to the church would still be fresh.

"Epiphany is the season of light, remember?" I said. "What better time to put up a lit tree than when everyone else has taken their lights down?"

"And we could switch out the coloured Christmas lights to white ones. Sell white bulbs," the idea person added, her voice rising in excitement.

The remaining details took a surprisingly short time to work out: when to put the tree up, when to take it down, who would oversee the project (idea woman), install the lights (husband), assemble the names in memory of, develop a small service (me, of course). We all agreed it was a pretty simple project.

The service was held in the evening, a few days after Epiphany. I debated whether I should read the names on the "in memory of" list inside the church, where it was warm, or out by the tree. I asked the idea woman for her opinion.

The church was filled as the first prayers began. People from five surrounding communities and some from a neighbouring parish sat pressed against one another in the narrow wooden pews.

There were trays of cookies not quite hidden here and there in the cramped space. Mugs and thermoses of hot chocolate waited on a back shelf.

Mid-way through the service, I led the people out into the night. Those who could manage walked up the steep hill toward the little spruce tree now filled with glowing white lights.

Flip the switch on before or after the names were read? Visibility had favoured the former.

Some helped others up the hill. Those too unsteady or fearful of falling stood in a semi-circle at the base, looking up.

Idea woman stood on one side of the tree. She read the names out slowly one by one, correctly pronouncing each one. *So glad I don't have that job*, I thought. She read loudly so everyone could hear. Her husband stood slightly over and behind her, shining a bright flashlight on the names.

I stood on the other side of the glowing tree, looking down over the people clustered on the hillside. Just dark shapes, no one distinguishable in the night. I looked beyond them to the bay, also dark. The full moon was out and a silver path spread across the water. *Light in the darkness,* I thought, turning toward the tree.

God in the Budget

"You can't do that!" the other minister said, his voice rising as he leaned across the table toward me, oblivious to the customers now turning to look at us.

Not a particularly private place to be having this conversation, I thought. But then who expected such a reaction? I set my Tim Horton's mug down carefully on the metal table.

"And why not?" I asked, leaning in as well. *Back off, buddy. I don't care if you're a colleague. Have some respect.*

"Because it's not fiscally responsible." I had forgotten until this moment that he had once been an accountant. Damn. What did I know about balance sheets and bottom lines compared to him?

"Maybe not. But it's theologically sound," I countered.

This conversation, which had started so civilly and with such good intentions, was spinning out of control.

'Twas the season of parish budgeting. I knew how the council was going to approach it this year with the new "no deficit budgeting allowed" guideline being implemented by the diocese. That's why I had asked him to meet with me. I wanted to test our plan with another clergy.

"Just so I am clear about this and so are you," my colleague said, taking a long sip of coffee, "you know you can't submit a negative budget, Right? That's diocesan policy."

"Right." I knew that.

"That means," he continued, obviously sensing that he was speaking to a financial dimwit, "you have to show where you are getting the monies that you expect to spend in your proposed budget."

"But we are going to show where the monies come from," I said calmly. How he would react was up in the air. "We know, for example, that there will be a shortfall of $15,000 as we go forward." I paused, took a bite from my muffin. "That's after we've included all the regular income from fundraising, envelopes, special offerings, rentals of the hall. We're including a line item under income in our budget that will take care of that. We're calling it …" My voice was drowned out by a new surge of customers heading up to the counter.

But my colleague had caught my last words. That's when the explosion happened, and not of the fruit muffin kind.

I hadn't always thought of finances the way I did now. In fact, once upon a time, I had thought much like my fellow rector sitting across from me. One person's faith had turned me around. I smiled slightly at the thought of Nancy.

Nancy, superintendent of the parish Sunday School. Nancy, bubbling over with enthusiasm for anything new or creative in the church, like clown ministry, for example. She'd been the best clown I'd ever seen, jumping up on a pew at the children's service last Christmas Eve, two toilet paper rolls taped together in makeshift binoculars as she peered out into an imaginary fog bank, looking for land and the Christ child. Nancy, with her great sense of humour and her belly-shaking laughter. Nancy, a woman my own age with an unstoppable faith in God's largesse.

The cups clattered all around us. My colleague was waiting for an explanation.

And all I could think of was that first difficult Advent season in the parish when I was learning my professional craft by the seat of my pants, and finances didn't figure very high on the list of my priorities.

The council meeting that December changed everything. That's when I found out how far in the red we really were: twelve thousand dollars owing in outstanding allotment (church tax), besides the regular bills to be paid. *The congregation isn't large and it's blue collar,* I thought. *Where is the money going to come from?* I started lying awake long into each night, looking up at the ceiling and coming up with absolutely nothing.

One afternoon, Nancy showed up at my door to discuss the Christmas pageant. She took one look at my pale face and asked, "What's up? Something seems to be bothering you." It all came pouring out—the worry and the lack of monies and time running out and…. I remembered clearly what Nancy said to me. It was something every minister needed to hear but seldom did. Something I've passed on to any students sent to me for training.

She looked at me for a full minute, smiled slowly, and said, "Stop worrying. God has always provided for this church and God always will."

My own disbelieving look only spurred Nancy on.

"You think this year is bad? We've had years when we were twice as far in the hole. But every year, the money comes in, to… the…penny. Every year our bills are paid by year-end. We never have anything left over to start the New Year, but we don't owe anything either. I can't explain it other than God comes through for us."

God was actually interested in something so tangible, so all-pervasive, as finances? My Scottish heritage whispered: *Nope, got to take care of that yourself. God helps those who help themselves, remember?*

"Now, stop worrying," Nancy said. "Have some faith, woman!" Cheeky comment to a minister!

So I stopped worrying. It wasn't doing me any good anyway. I decided to trust both Nancy's wisdom and God. Did I or did I not believe in the Scriptures, the lilies of the field and all that? I knew I couldn't add a cubit to my height; I'd tried since I was a child. I waited to see what would happen. I had a great Christmas.

I wondered, as I added a bit more sugar to my coffee, if my friend across from me was sleeping well these days. Especially if he only thought in terms of numbers and bottom lines?

Because Nancy had been right. New Year's Eve arrived that first year. The bills were all paid, the regular ones and the outstanding allotment. The money came in largely on the offering plate. Only a few dollars remained in the parish account. The church was starting the year with a clean slate.

The same scenario had happened every year in the eight years since.

This year it was finally time to put down on paper what we all knew to be true in my parish. What Nancy, one of our most illustrious souls, had taught me.

"Some of us live in the real world," my colleague said, as he pushed back his chair and stood.

"Our parish budget this year lists the item *God Provides* with the shortfall beside it," I told him firmly.

"Let's just see what happens. Maybe meet up this time next year to talk about it?"

Entertaining Angels Unaware

Often the church is not good about being the Gospel or Good News to others. Ask someone who's left the church "Why?" and most likely, you'll hear a story about not being welcomed, being excluded and ignored, or being maligned. They're all too common. Most churchgoers have a file of their own stories. Yet strangers and regulars still come through the doors looking for community and a place to belong, seeking evidence or at least reflections of the Ultimate Reality, the Holy One of Israel, the Christ.

Abraham sat at the door of his tent under the Mamre oaks, watching three figures approach. Everything that followed hung on an act of hospitality. Everything still does.

Memory: A Student's Perspective

There are many ways to exclude.

We speak a different language in churches, not only Elizabethan English at times, but in acronyms. Would someone please tell newcomers or irregular regulars what BCP and BAS and BHB and RHB and CP and HC and MP mean?

She was a slight woman with short, dark blonde hair, in her mid-forties. There was an air of quiet about her.

Was this her first time at service?

I wondered, as I noticed her, if someone had helped her with the books. We had an abundance: hymn books (the red United/Anglican one, the ancient blue hymnal from when I was a child, the new Common Praise one with the inclusive language the choir objected to, the Mission and Praise one the organist made fun of), two prayer books, and part of the service was printed in the bulletin. Even if you were used to worshipping here, it could be confusing.

And what did the newcomer think of all the standing, kneeling, and sitting? The clergy in charge of the service didn't give liturgical instructions. It interrupted the flow of worship, he said. I couldn't see much from my assigned seating in the choir. But I thought she sat at the back so at least she had the congregation to follow.

I'd met her a few weeks before. I had answered the parish phone and she'd left a message. Could she get help with some groceries?

I checked out her situation. The one-room apartment was in an old Victorian house, close to the church, and contained all her worldly possessions. She had recently left a bad marriage. "I used to belong to a women's group in church. It was the one place I was allowed to go on my own," she told me. "But they collected dues and I had no money of my own, so I dropped out." We sat enveloped by threadbare overstuffed chairs and talked for hours. Two women, roughly the same age. Vastly different lives.

What had it taken for her to walk up the stone steps of the church that morning, open the great oak door, come in? Most people we helped didn't ever come to worship.

Coffee hour was one of my favourite times in the week. There was good conversation. Good food, too, but don't bring a store-bought pie as your contribution; they won't serve it.

After the service, the congregation moved downstairs into

a rectangular common area. Several older women stood filling cups at the kitchen pass-thru. The noise level was rising, as well as the temperature. A few kids ran among all the legs. What must we look like from that vantage point? The corners of the room were filling with various groupings.

And there she was, coming down the stairs. She was on her own. I was alone too. No family with me on that Sunday; such is the life of a student.

I was also still unsettled because of what had happened during the service.

I had leaned forward over the altar rail to offer the chalice when the woman before me (grey-haired pillar of the church) looked up and recoiled as if she had seen a snake. I almost lost my grip on the cup. Now wouldn't that have been a mess?

I approached the woman at the beginning of coffee hour to check out her reaction. But she was talking to some friends and she kept on talking until I stepped away. No sense rocking the boat—or the chalice for that matter—over something so little. Still, it stung.

Coffee hour was gradually wrapping up. In the midst of the swirling groups, laughter, plans being made, coffee cups emptying I saw the newcomer standing alone, a still point in all the chaos, waiting.

There are many ways to exclude.

Feeding the Hungry

The food bank sat on the edge of the metro area, and covered a lot of territory. It fed more than forty families every two weeks. A few families had two people, but most had four to six, sometimes more.

Someone in the church had had the idea of helping in a tangible way decades before, and the need had grown each year since: school age children, toddlers, teens, live-at-home twenty-somethings, seniors being cared for at home by their children, a lot of the sandwich generation, single family parents, people off their meds, people battling addictions, the unemployed, the working poor. The other clergy in the area didn't support it, saying it "perpetuated dependency." Their congregations had a different perspective. Direction and oversight of the food bank was shared jointly with leaders from all the surrounding churches.

On a food bank day, chairs were lined up around the edges of the large church hall, and people spoke in low tones. Men dressed in go-to-church clothes, women in polyester slacks, oversized T-shirts, and sweaters. One by one, they made their way up to the desk set in the middle of the room to give their trackable information.

Just before the bags of groceries were given out, clients and leaders would gather in one great circle, hold hands and say a prayer. It didn't seem out of place here, where many people had been raised by strong moms with strong faiths. Any who didn't believe in a loving God took their place in the circle and held hands, too.

A few years back, the Sunday School planted a garden out behind the hall. One server noticed how little fresh stuff was on offer from the metro food bank, and suggested a parish garden. It sat just outside the back door of the hall, clearly visible from the highway, its raised bed a tangle of tomatoes, Swiss chard, carrots, and yellow and green beans. Despite the naysayers—always a few of those around—and their prediction that it would be vandalized, the garden thrived. Church gardeners pitched in and a few of us less talented souls who knew how to weed helped out. Part of each year, fresh produce poked out of the bags of tinned veggies and meat. The children planted the seeds and the adults saw the harvest.

Ellen was the quiet one sitting at the food bank table. She

noticed details. She found out who needed school supplies, a warm blanket, a heater, and countless other things about those who sat around the edges. She made sure they got what they needed, and did it anonymously.

Her slow smile lit up a room.

Shortly after we met, I asked how she spent her days now that she was retired. I listened to her long response. Then I asked, "Do you have any life outside the church?" She smiled.

When a going away party was held in her honour, there wasn't room on the cake to list all the ministries she was part of. She was a lay reader, chalice bearer, sang in the choir, read Scripture in church, occasionally preached, greeted people at the door, took part in prison ministry, led a Monday evening Bible study and a Bethel group, was a member of parish council. And of course, there was the food bank.

Oh, what a party that turned out to be. People from the surrounding communities, churchgoers, family and friends poured into the balloon-decorated hall. Tables sat in front of the stage, heaped with food. Different musical groups and fiddlers played through the afternoon.

She had been diagnosed with Lou-Gehrig's Disease a few months before. As she learned more about what to expect, it became clear that she had to move in with her daughter in another province, far away from the church she loved and from all her friends. She started to wrap up her ministries one by one. She began the long list of goodbyes.

Bit by bit she was losing herself. Not her mind, but most everything else.

On her last Sunday in the parish, she presented herself at the altar, prepared to administer the chalice.

We had talked about her continuing this ministry. "But I can't say the words you're supposed to say over each person," she said.

"You don't need the words," I said, thinking, *They need you offering the cup.*

As I looked up from the altar, I saw her and the person assigned to the job that day. Two people: one chalice. She had mixed up the schedule.

Administering the bread during Communion was a particularly sacred time for me and one I was not prone to share, but that day I gave her the bread.

She bent over the rail, placed torn off pieces into hands. So many hands that day were lifted up to her. Hands that had shared ministries with her over the years, hands that had received food and blankets and care baskets from her, hands that had prayed with her about others, hands she had comforted with her own, hands joined in a great unbroken circle.

Against All Odds

It was an odd request, I thought. Yet it should be the norm, considering the nature of my work.

We were sitting at the local greasy spoon, having coffee and discussing the church, as was our regular Monday morning practice. He was a key leader in the parish faith community. A slim, beautifully dressed businessman about ten years older than me. I respected his opinions. In my difficult work as a newbie rector, he'd never steered me wrong.

Now here he was, asking something of me. "Look," he said, "I really don't know where it all went off-track with her. You know her. She comes to church every week. We used to be friends, her and her husband, me and my wife."

I nodded, knowing who he meant.

"I don't know what I did to hurt her. She won't speak to me. When it comes to the passing of the peace, she looks right through me. She leaves the altar rail when I offer the cup."

The pain in his voice was piercing.

"I've tried talking to her, but she turns away. I can't even apologize. It's tearing me up inside."

Here was a man who believed in the soul, and in justice, but mostly he believed in the power of reconciliation. I knew this from the past few months, working with him, seeing him work with others in the church, seeing the look on his face as he stood at the rail offering the wine and saying, "The blood of Christ, shed for you."

The server poured more coffee into my half-filled cup. I stirred in the cream, watched it dissipate.

"And how can I help you?" I asked slowly, knowing what he would say but not wanting to hear it.

"Can you go see her? Tell her I know I've hurt her. Tell her that I'm sorry. Then at least I will have done my best by her."

He understood what needed to happen when there's a breakdown in a relationship in the church family, I thought. Hurt, forgiveness, and reconciliation were powerful forces that few people understood.

There was the naming of the hurt, the assumption of responsibility by one party at least, and the apology with no expectation of forgiveness. It was up to the person who had been hurt to decide to forgive or not. Forgiveness had to come from a position of power, or it was not authentic. Even the church had been guilty of demanding their people forgive at all costs, forgetting that some hurts take a lifetime to process. Apologize, forgive, shake hands now and everything will go back to the way it once was—relationships don't work that way.

I didn't know what to say as I sat across from him, hearing his agony.

One bright winter's day not long after our discussion, I found myself walking up the steps to the sprawling old farmhouse where she lived. My heart was beating fast. *Please God*, I prayed silently as I rang the doorbell, *please God*. It was tricky approaching someone who was a regular churchgoer about something so tender. It could explode in my face.

It did. The woman's anger sprayed the room. "How dare you come here and talk about this?" she demanded. I shrank back in my chair, trying to still the shaking china cup in my hand. I swallowed a few times and then ventured, "Actually, I'm here simply to pass on a message. He wants you to know that he is very sorry about the hurt he's caused you. That's all."

That's everything, I thought, and, *there would be fewer feuds spanning generations in the church if we took this work seriously.*

After a few more uncomfortable minutes, the visit ended. I walked back to my car, wondering if anything at all had been accomplished.

Two weeks later, just before service, I was crossing the parking lot to the church building. There, almost hidden between two cars, stood my key leader and the woman. They were talking.

As far as I ever knew, the two never regained their former good relationship. But the woman no longer left the altar rail when he served the wine. "This is my blood, poured out for you." They looked at each other during the passing of the peace.

Anyone For a Lift?

Why is it that some intelligent, usually caring, people just can't put themselves in someone else's shoes? Or wheelchair? It makes me want to shove them into one and make them stay there for a full day, to see how others see them, to see where the real obstacles are.

Take the exclusion of Peter, for example.

Peter was a parish lay reader. Despite being confined to a wheelchair, he carried out his church duties with joy and grace and seldom missed a service. He was at church early on Sundays, gowned and waiting to help the rector around the altar.

Sometimes he managed two services, travelling from one end of the parish to the other, hefting himself from van to chair, and up sometimes slippery wheelchair ramps with the help of his wife.

Every month or so one of the churches would host a social following the service. These were times of coming together, exchanging stories and gossip and family news, and bonding with neighbours and friends. Kids ran around in packs, sat at their own tables. The most senior churchgoers usually sat in chairs arranged around the edges of the room, waited upon by the middle aged and the younger seniors. There was always a crush of people staffing the kitchen, offering coffee and tea at the pass-thru, cooking and flipping whatever was on order, washing dishes. It was a noisy, chaotic time. Everyone was invited whether they were newcomer, or regular, or visitor.

The problem was that all socials were held in the basements of the two churches. Neither was wheelchair accessible. Peter couldn't come.

Council listened carefully to my suggestion that at least one church install a chair lift down the stairwell.

"Why can't we just carry him down?" one member said.

"Yup, we can do that. We've got strong men here," another added.

"How would you feel being carried downstairs by someone else?" I asked. No response. I remembered my mother-in-law being carried downstairs to a social event in another church, her frightened face peering out from between burly arms. *There's fear, and there's dignity,* I thought.

"It's going to cost a lot," someone said.

"Can someone check out prices and the actual dimensions needed and report back?" I asked. Someone volunteered to do so.

Six months later the discussion was still ongoing. I tried to underscore my impatience by sitting upstairs with Peter during socials, rather than going downstairs with the others. No one noticed.

Several things then happened in quick succession.

First, an elderly woman in the parish fell, coming up the uneven stairs in one church. Fortunately, she fell on the landing, so it was just unnerving to those around her rather than dangerous. That did it. The church wardens agreed the time had come to remove the stairs and build new ones to code. The stairwell would be under construction for months. *A perfect opportunity to introduce a wheelchair lift,* I thought.

Second, council was informed that a past parishioner had died and left some money to the same church. It would more than cover the new stairwell and a lift.

Still council hesitated.

"Such a lot of money to spend for just one person," some members said.

"The congregation's getting older and some would already use the lift if there was one," I countered, thinking furiously, *So what if it's just one person? It might be you if you develop a knee problem or break a leg.*

"He's the only one who will use it. No one else will, and it's still a lot of money."

In the end, they decided to go ahead with the project. It cost much more than a chair lift in an ordinary home because this was a church and therefore had to be to code for a public place. *Interesting,* I thought, *when a home lift gets much more use.*

The first day it was used was when the bishop came for his yearly visit. The bishop sat in the lift's chair and pressed the button. He waved at those watching from below, and declared it a smooth, comfortable ride. Then Peter took his place. His wife waited at the bottom with his wheelchair.

"We should get one of those lightweight wheelchairs for the church," I heard someone say behind me.

Peter came up to me later, and said gruffly, "First social I've been to here in decades." He wiped his eyes.

We held a dedication service for the new lift. I knew that what was about to happen would blow the roof off. Or at least I hoped it would.

I had prepared for the service carefully. I had gone to see the family of the woman who had left the money to the church. No conditions had been imposed on how the church could spend the bequest—*always a good thing*, I thought. But I hadn't expected the reaction of the daughter when I told her about the lift being dedicated in memory of her mom.

On the dedication Sunday, the daughter was sitting at the front with the children gathered in a semi-circle around her. Instead of a sermon on this special day, she was telling them a story. She told them about her mom who had always loved going to this church. Her mom had gone to Sunday School here, had taught Sunday School, had sung in the choir, and helped out with all sorts of church events. "But then one day," the daughter said, "she couldn't come anymore. Do you know why?" The children shook their heads vigorously. She had the congregation's complete attention.

"She got sick and weak. She couldn't get up the stairs into the church anymore. In those days, you didn't have a ramp here. She spent the last years of her life in a wheelchair, largely housebound. She spent those years missing her church. And that's why this is such a fitting memorial for her. This chair makes it possible for everyone to take part in everything."

The stillness in the church was profound.

The celebration that day was everything you could wish for. Chaos and laughter, everyone downstairs, and some asking about this woman they remembered from years ago before she got sick. The daughter was surrounded by kids, and some of them took her to the lift and invited her to ride up and down on it. And then they did, too.

Toward the end of the social, I took one of the church wardens upstairs into the main worship area and said, "I'm leaving soon, so I can only suggest this project I've been thinking about. See this space that's not being used?" I led him to a large open area just inside an emergency door and just outside the vestry room. It was tucked around the corner, out of sight of the congregation.

"It wouldn't take much, you know, to install a bathroom here that would be wheelchair accessible. The one downstairs is too small to adapt that way. And you could easily install a ramp directly outside the emergency door. I think there's enough money left over to do that. What do you think?"

"Well, I don't know," he said, measuring out his words carefully. "It would cost a lot. Not many people would use it."

No New Members

The catering group in the church wondered why no one wanted to join their ranks. They were getting tired, and each year their numbers were smaller. They finally came up with an answer, which they shared with me. "People come and help out for one dinner and that's it. They don't come back, not after they find out how much work is involved."

I had a different idea, which I wanted to test out first, just to be sure.

I volunteered for kitchen duty at the next supper. They were pleased I wanted to help out.

When a group's been working together as long as this one has, I thought, *it will be hard to accommodate someone new in the kitchen.* Was that part of the problem? I was curious where they would put me.

They assigned me to slice tomatoes. Each one had to be sliced in exactly seven slices in order not to exceed the number of tomatoes we had for the number of plates expected. No one told me that. Halfway through the dinner, we ran out of tomatoes.

The next dinner, having learned their lesson re tomato slices, they assigned me to the gravy station. The station was located at one end of the kitchen pass-thru, so anyone looking up from any table in the dining area would see their minister there.

The gravy station was the last stop in the roast beef dinner assembly line, after the meat, potatoes, green beans, and carrots had been carefully arranged on each plate. I was instructed to dip the ladle in the big gravy pot, and pour its contents—two thirds full so as not to run out—over the meat and the potatoes. *Mentorship is a wonderful thing*, I thought, as I confidently ladled gravy out onto plates.

Ten minutes into the dinner and countless plates later, someone pulled me off the station.

"What are you doing?" the woman standing in front of me demanded in an exasperated tone. "You're sending out cold gravy on those plates!"

That day I learned that there is a technique for ladling gravy out of pots. Dip down to the bottom (where the hot gravy is), pull up to the top (past colder gravy), and pour. This also stirs the gravy. Pity no one had mentioned it to me before.

Now I knew that there was a technique for not attracting new members. The question was, would I stir it all up or not?

Across Old Divides

"The Blessing of the Fishing Fleet is a long-standing tradition," the Baptist minister told me a few weeks after I was in my new parish. "We alternate locations. This year you're hosting it and we're providing the music—a fishermen's a cappella choir."

The Baptist and Anglican churches faced each other across an intersection down by the bay. Every direction from there led to fishing villages. The two congregations didn't mingle much on a Sunday morning. Who would have guessed they would come together for a Blessing of the Fishing Fleet service each year?

Despite the rather short notice, everything came together in time. On the night of the service, our small church filled up with local fishermen. Brightly coloured buoys were piled up against the base of the altar. The men's voices, including their pastor's, carried me out across the waters and back to another sea in the Holy Land.

The social that followed in our church basement was dubbed a success by everyone who came. "Some of my flock aren't here tonight," the Baptist pastor confided over his coffee cup. "They just aren't prepared yet." I wondered what he meant.

A month before the next Blessing was scheduled, the pastor appeared on the rectory doorstep with a written statement for me. "I warned you it would come to this," he began.

What is he talking about? I thought, frantically trying to recall him saying anything of the sort.

"I told you that your church's stance on the blessing of same-sex unions would be a problem."

Oh...that...

"I told you I couldn't, in good conscience, be part of any cooperation between our two churches if it went in this direction. I presented this statement to my board of elders last night and they agree with me." He handed me the paper.

"But here's where the Anglican Church in this diocese stands," I told him, producing the bishop's recent statement. He glanced at it quickly. Was he actually reading it? I couldn't tell.

"And you can see that no decision has been made."

Why was I responding this way instead of saying out loud what my heart had already concluded and he was perhaps sensing: my personal opinion and the official stance of the church were at odds. Why had my mom taught me to be so damned polite? All I wanted to do was push him out the door and slam it behind him. ("A slammed door is an admission of defeat," my mom's quiet voice said in my head. "Go away!" I said back.)

He didn't look convinced.

A week later, he announced to his congregation that he would be away the night of the service; they could participate if they wanted to. And so ended a long-observed tradition between the Baptists and the Anglicans.

Or so I thought.

I had often wondered why the Roman Catholic Church, just a few kilometers down the road, wasn't part of the service. The answer I kept getting from some of my lay leaders and from the Baptist pastor was, "They're not interested."

I decided to invite their priest anyway—a younger man who was overseeing the parish from a nearby city. He came out on weekends for services and for pastoral care. He was his bishop's ecumenical relations officer as well, tasked with improving relations between different churches. He was pleased with the invitation. As far as he knew, no one had ever invited them to participate. So much for the sources I had listened to.

Once again, the Anglican Church hosted the Blessing of the Fishing Fleet service and the turnout was good. Quite a few people identified themselves as members of the Catholic Church. The priest and I shared the prayers and he preached. *What a good sermon*, I thought. *Relevant and interesting.* I noticed the fishermen, all listening intensely. The social afterward was considered a success by all who came. Only two people showed up from the Baptist church across the intersection.

October rolled around. A new Baptist pastor arrived in the area, replacing the one who had opted out the previous November. *Wonder what he's like?* I thought. I dropped in on him and his wife to extend a welcome from the Anglicans in the area.

Unpacked boxes were stacked everywhere. Books covered

any available flat surface. We sat in the midst of the chaos in the kitchen, getting to know each other.

It was now or never. "What would you think about participating in the Blessing of the Fleet service next month?" I asked him. I began filling him in on the long tradition, recently adjusted to be more denominationally inclusive. Perhaps, I added at the end of our chat, we could all meet together—he and I and the Roman Catholic priest—and discuss how we might approach the service with three congregations involved. He was intrigued.

On the first Tuesday evening of November, we assembled with our people to say prayers over the fishermen and their gear. Very early the next morning the boats would head out into the icy waters of the Bay of Fundy, piled high with lobster traps. Laying them down and hauling them in was dangerous, backbreaking, freezing labour. Most years one or two fishermen along the bay didn't come back.

Just up from the pier where the fishing boats were moored, the doors of the small Roman Catholic Church stood wide open, despite the chill of the night. Cars were lined up and down the narrow village road, making it hard to find a spot to park. The hall across the road from the church was lit up; its doors open to accommodate the stream of people bringing in covered dishes and platters for the social afterward. *They go all-out here,* I thought.

Ten minutes before service and the pews were full: Anglicans, Baptists, and Roman Catholics out in full force. Someone brought in extra chairs and even then, people were standing at the back, pressed up against the door. Expectation pulsed in the air.

"We're so pleased to be hosting tonight's Blessing of the Fishing Fleet for the very first time," the priest began. A few individuals began to clap to a lot of broad grins.

I looked down from where I was sitting, out over the faces. There were fishermen, a lot of them, and their families; the men's choir from the Baptist church; one of our young violinists who would be offering a solo tonight; people I'd waved to on my way to visit parishioners.

"We're out there working side by side on the water," a fisherman told me at the reception later. "It's only right to be worshipping together."

Fishing gear spilled up the aisle and around the altar. A banner was prominently mounted to one side, featuring Peter, patron saint of fishermen. Candles flickered beside the altar.

My throat constricted. *This is how it should be, should always have been.* The three of us stood side by side behind the altar as everyone began singing the old hymns that had been sung in separate churches for a hundred years. We stood as the Gospel passage was read about some fishermen long ago, plying their trade on another sea. The new Baptist pastor moved to the pulpit and began his sermon.

"Once upon a time," he said, smiling out at the people and back at us, "there was an Anglican minister, a Roman Catholic priest and a Baptist pastor who were out fishing in a boat."

The Lines We Cross

All I could see was red. This was not a good sign. Red is for rage. Red is for warning. Red is for stop before you get run over by something coming at you sideways.

My archdeacon was speaking to me. His words were being drowned out by the pounding of blood in my ears. I tried hard to slow my breathing and unclench my hands.

It was a simple request. He wanted me to go after the people who had just left my parish—the twelve key leaders who had resigned two months before and taken their abilities elsewhere. He had chaired the meeting on the night they slapped down their Out Of Here letters in front of the whole parish. That explosive night had shattered the parish and it had shattered me.

Since then, everyone left behind had worked hard at filling the leadership gaps. People were stepping forward, and different takes on old ministries were being tried. Some people who had never volunteered before were doing so and enjoying it. A new energy and attitude flowed through the church.

"Why would you ask that?" I managed to say, trying to control my tone.

"I've been talking to Elmer," he said, naming the clergy who had been my parish's rector several rectors before me. "He says you haven't even tried to go after them. And that they're hurt."

Right. Of course Elmer would be concerned. This was the group he had pulled together in the first place, raised up to leadership, encouraged in their ministries. (*Foisted on future ministers,* my worse side whispered.)

"Your parish can't afford to lose them," the archdeacon continued, "in more ways than one. So I'd like you to go after them."

It wasn't the first time a former rector had stepped into my area of responsibility. But it was the worst case so far.

In seminary, I hadn't been taught about the dangers of interfering in a parish once you left. It might have been the subject of a case study or two, but there were no written rules concerning interference, so far as I knew. Canon law did not address it, nor did the bishop's guidelines for proper clergy behaviour.

Yet everyone understands that some things just aren't done, don't they? Isn't this Clergy Relations 101 stuff?

Don't they teach you this in archdeacon school? I thought, looking hard at my archdeacon.

Apparently not. I stalked out of his office that day, promising I'd get back to him. *How many lines were just crossed in our conversation?* I wondered as I drove home.

* * *

In the years since, I have discovered that what once seemed so clear to me no longer is. Maybe it's because I'm more seasoned. Or less territorial. Or because now I realize how blurred the lines can be between the past and the present when it comes to relationships with past parishioners.

"It's easy to get in trouble even if you do nothing," I told my bishop over coffee one day. I was thinking about two incidents with rectors of parishes where I had once served.

The first was rather serious. A former leader of a woman's group was dying. She had a special place in my heart for her positive outlook, deep faith, and great sense of humour. After I left the parish, we stayed in touch. Her family called me one day, more than a decade after I had stopped being her priest.

"Jane would like to see you. Can you come?" her daughter asked.

"I'll check in with Jane's priest first," I said, hoping I'd get the go-ahead on the visit. It would be good to see her and tell her how much of a difference she'd made in my life. Too often I didn't get the chance to say goodbye.

Her current rector gave me permission to visit with no hesitation.

I sat holding Jane's hand beside the hospital bed the family had installed in her living room. We talked of the past, and of her family and her grandchildren, and of what might lie ahead. I said a prayer and I said goodbye.

Ten days later and I woke to the phone ringing very early in the morning. *Must be an emergency,* I thought, stumbling to reach it in time.

Jane's priest was on the line. She was finding it difficult to articulate; not a good sign. Finally she got it out.

"Jane has died."

"Okay?" Not unexpected.

"The funeral's set for here, on Saturday at two."

"Thanks for letting me know." Most clergy wouldn't have bothered.

"Did you," the words were spaced out now, "tell Jane's family that you would… preach…at…her… service?"

I hadn't talked to Jane's family the day of the visit at all except for a brief greeting on my way to the living room.

"Of course not," I said carefully. "And they didn't ask if I would, either," I added. "I would have referred them back to you if they had."

"You're sure?" the rector said. "I've had other clergy that made such offers in the past, undermining my role."

I couldn't go to Jane's funeral because I was officiating at one myself that day. I knew Jane would understand. It might have been tricky showing up in any case.

The second incident was minor, but potentially attitude-shifting nevertheless.

I had just retired and was finding the sudden withdrawal from parish life difficult, so I jumped at the chance to have coffee in a local shop with a friend and former parishioner. We mostly talked of family. I listened as she talked about current happenings in the parish, monitoring my few responses carefully. It was hard not to be interested in the work going on in a place I once served with all my heart. It was hard not to have opinions.

The inner monologue was unending. *Not my concern now, don't step over the line, don't comment, listen and refer her back to the current rector, you know this.*

It was hard to cut the ties. It helped that I liked the new rector and thought him a good choice for the parish. Still, would I have reacted any differently to a poor choice? I knew what kinds of problems an interfering or overly opinionated clergy could make for a new rector.

We wrapped up our conversation and I went home, pleased with my stellar restraint.

The phone rang in my study early the next evening. It was the new rector.

"Hi," I said. It was good to hear his voice.

"Hi," he replied. "Got to ask you something I don't want to ask."

"Shoot," I said, wondering what was up.

"Did you meet with Betty this week for coffee?"

"Yes," I said, puzzled. I wondered if I shouldn't have.

"This is difficult." Long pause. "Did you tell her you'd be preaching at my induction?" The service was only a few weeks away.

"No. I wouldn't do that."

"Oh," he said sounding vastly relieved, "that's good. I already have someone else lined up. Betty told my wife you were doing that and my wife relayed it on to me saying, 'I think you have a conflict.'"

We have liftoff, Houston!

"She just wasn't listening carefully," I said, finally making the connections. "I did tell her I was delighted you had invited me to the service, which isn't usually done."

And that's how easily things can go off-track between a former and a current rector.

I now know there has to be a cut-off point when a priest leaves a parish: you can go this far and no further without damaging another's ability to do effective ministry in your wake.

Parishioners find that difficult to understand. Some may always see you as their priest, because of the heart-rending or joyful times you have shared. Some will compare the new rector to you as you were compared to the one you succeeded.

A heart's alliance isn't shifted easily. It takes time. Hence the cut-off rule that every clergy is supposed to know, but no one has written down. Sometimes the heart that needs to move on is your own.

* * *

I called my archdeacon as soon as I got home. "I've thought it over," I said defiantly. "I'm not going after them. They've already moved on. The parish has too."

You Can Never Go Back

Beloved people of past lives,
circles almost touching circles,
everything in its season
the spaces between so small but there
bubbles rising in a glass.

The invite was too intriguing to pass up. My retirement days hadn't held a lot of invites. Now I had been invited back to my home parish's 50th anniversary.

On the drive there, memories surfaced, thick and fast. The partial ones—like the young minister leaning over the end of pew whispering, "Thy child stinketh," on the one day I didn't have my diaper bag. The fumes drifting up from the playpen at the back as he spoke. The full-blown, glow-in-the-dark ones—my Beloved's first sermon as a lay reader; the day the new minister came to town (a woman).

How many people would I still know? How many would be gone, moved away, or buried in the local cemetery? I hadn't kept in touch, busy as I was, involved with other parishes, other commitments, life. Would anyone remember me? I flipped down the visor mirror. *Probably not.*

From the outside, it still looked the same, other than new

glass doors. Two women from long ago greeted me like they used to—they grinned and hugged me close. *And here I thought I wouldn't know anyone.* There were familiar faces in the pews, up front in the choir, sitting beside me, behind me. "In memory of" lines in the bulletin listed some who had died. I hadn't known.

So much was new here, and rearranged. So much was the same. Cutting-edge music by the band offset old traditional hymns. Other people from the past kept coming through the door: former rectors and spouses, former students, former parishioners. No one looked much older. I still recognized them and, shockingly, some recognized me.

It'd be great fun to come here to worship, I thought. *Too far,* my saner self reminded me. *But still, I could come back here if I had the time. Begin again differently, be welcomed, find my place.*

* * *

"You can never go back," the bishop said as we finished up lunch. "You know that, don't you?"

It had been six months since my retirement and I was missing community. I was missing the feel of standing behind an altar, beginning the Great Thanksgiving prayer. I was missing the eclectic band music that was a bright point of worship. I was missing familiar faces and belonging somewhere I loved. I was drifting out to sea, like a dory that had become unmoored.

"Of course I know that," I said quickly.

My heart just hadn't figured it out yet.

"Give the parish a year, and we can go back," I told my husband, who was grieving too. That was the standard length of time recommended to outgoing clergy.

My interpretation of the unwritten rule went something like this: Give the new priest a year to establish himself, then I could go back. I'd just sit in the pew beside my husband and enjoy the worship. I could even offer to help a bit here and there. Other parishes have retired clergy and it worked for them.

I knew better. I'd seen the aftermath of what happened when a past rector was too close. Mostly, it wasn't pretty. It got ugly sometimes.

I'd listened to retired clergy who were terribly upset at not being used in worship or not being included in activities. Watched as their self-esteem washed away, waiting for an invitation that never came, or came too seldom.

I'd seen current and former rectors disagreeing on issues privately and sometimes in public. What a mess.

I can't go back. The bishop was right. Maybe for the occasional visit, but certainly not permanently. My heart ached thinking about it.

Then we went back.

We decided to surprise Bert, and just drop in on him without calling first. We were in the city for a visit, close to a parish I'd served a few years before.

He was a former warden of mine, a big man with a pragmatic, open heart. He'd stood beside me during a church demolition, and during the mass exodus of our parish's leadership. His insight and sheer force of perseverance kept me from leaving that awful first year. We'd shovelled gravel together, shovelled out crap at council meetings, and sometimes cried about the terrible things people do to one another. We'd laughed a lot too. He knew I was the right one, he once told me, on the night the selection committee interviewed me.

After I left, he'd call occasionally just to talk. He'd let me know someone had died, or that there was no new minister yet, or ask if I was happy where I was. When he came to my city, a full day's trip for him, I'd meet him over lunch to get caught up. He never seemed to change.

We set out for his place, driving down familiar roads. We

passed the rectory where we'd once lived, where so many meetings had been held, the setting of so many scenes. I noticed a car parked in its now-paved driveway.

We turned onto Bert's road, parked, walked up his shingle-covered steps to the front door, rang the doorbell and waited. *Hope he's home,* I thought, and then, *He must be. His car is here.*

A stranger opened the door. *Has he moved?* I wondered. We asked for him and were ushered into the large country kitchen. Bert sat at one end of the kitchen table that dominated the room. I remembered drinking mugs of coffee at this table as we pondered parish problems.

He looked up, surprised. *He doesn't know who I am,* my heart whispered.

"Hi, Bert, it's Bonnie," I said, my lips stretched in a smile. "You remember my husband. We were in the area and thought we'd stop by. Hope you don't mind."

We introduced ourselves to the visiting relatives in the kitchen. We told a few stories about ministering together in the parish and the fine job he'd done as warden and in so many other capacities. I mentioned how we often thought of him.

After a half an hour or so, we turned to leave. We'd stayed just long enough to be polite. Bert hadn't said much. He just nodded now and then.

He walked us to the door and said, looking down at me, "You were always my favourite minister, you know."

"Must be the meds he's on," my husband said as we drove away, trying to minimize the impact. *Had he really remembered?* I wondered. Bert had always been good at figuring out things from little clues.

Nothing stays the same.

We dropped in somewhere else a few weeks later. The message on the parish phone said, "Services are at 9 am and 10:45." We showed up at 10:30, strolled up the cobbled front laneway, opened the door and walked into the last ten minutes of the service. No one had adjusted the message to reflect the one special service of the day.

Wow, I thought. *We missed the sermon, missed Communion, missed everything except the announcements.* I did have time to look around.

It wasn't so different from ten years before when we left. The riveting painting, which was the pride of the church, was in the same place. So was the altar and its new rail. It wasn't new any longer, I reminded myself. I recognized a lot of people in the choir and around the altar. The new minister, several months into his rectorship, seemed very much at home already.

A couple stood at the end of the pew, looking at us. They were probably back from setting up for coffee time after service, I thought. We both seemed to realize that this was their pew. His glasses sat on the book ledge. They continued to wait. With five minutes to go, we moved to the pew behind theirs. Some things don't change.

"We're having a meeting to discuss parish visioning, but there's a social beforehand. Come join us," the new minister offered generously. Why not? We decided we'd only stay a few moments.

The hall had a new paint job, and a new children's activity corner. *This is the place I learned to be a priest,* I thought. I'd learned to handle dicey council meetings, learned what happens if you make changes too fast with too little explanation, learned what happens when you back people into a corner. I'd also learned to laugh at myself, to trust in God's provision, and had seen absolution given in many ways.

Some of my teachers were no longer around. A few my age—and some a lot younger—were buried in the graveyard that flanked the church. Some were in the kitchen, setting out plates and emerging with hot dishes for the common table up front.

Others clustered around us as we walked in.

A woman I remembered pointed out another familiar figure across the room. "I'll go get her," she said.

She led Glenda by the hand. "This," she said to Glenda, "is Reverend Bonnie."

Glenda was an attractive woman about fifteen years or so older than me. She had always exuded confidence and goodwill. She had been, like Bert, one of my parish wardens and a valued mentor. I'd spent a lot of afternoons in her living room, drinking pots of tea, planning council meeting agendas or figuring out how to present difficult news to a church.

The woman turned to my husband. "And this is Bonnie's husband. Bonnie used to be your rector," she said.

"I have a hard time placing people," Glenda said, taking my offered hand. There was no shared memory in her eyes. Her unfailing confidence had taken a hit. She was meeting me for the first time.

Two people from the past. Sometimes the message is clear.

"You can never go back," the bishop said. My heart knows that now.

Maybe as a past parishioner, but not as a past clergy. It's too complicated. There is only the present.

Another name for gift.

So You Want to Be a Minister...

"So you want to be a minister," the formation director said, peering over his half glasses at us. That year, most of us were in our late thirties, or older. All women, for the first time in the school's Anglican history; second-career people. We knew how the real world worked. We were here to find out how the church worked, and how to be leaders in its alternate reality.

Year one at theological school turned out to be an eye opener.

"Well..." he said, "first of all you need to become aware of how you present yourself."

Presence, he's talking about presence, I thought, excitement beginning to build. *How to become still, conduct oneself during worship...* "To begin with," he continued, "I want you to think about what you are wearing...on your ears. And what that says about you to others."

I was wearing dangly green parrot earrings.

I can still remember reaching up and pulling those earrings out, cheeks hot, and wishing I could be anywhere else. I believed him. He was in the know, I wasn't.

"So you want to be a minister," the young man said as I drove him home from class on a bitterly cold night. "What kind of work did you do before? Or," he paused before adding, "did you work?"

I don't know why I answered.

"I see," he pronounced. "You went as far as you could in that career, and now you're here to prove you can do this too."

His comment still rankles and I don't know why. It was never about that.

Others in those years of training commented on what they considered to be essential matters for a proper clergy: no multicolored shoes peeking out from under your alb, no dyed red hair sticking up in spikes, no laughing like a hyena in the school dining room, no storytelling unless you fully explained your point, no one of your gender (a few of those in those days).

The real essentials were best articulated a few years later by a favourite minister. He'd been a crucial part of my spiritual life as a teen, someone I aspired to be like. I drove him to the airport one day, and on the way, I told him I would soon be priested. I knew he was probably not in favour of women priests, but I wanted his blessing.

"What do you think?" I asked, holding my breath.

He turned slightly toward me and said, "Don't do this unless you want to do it with all your heart. It will take all your strength and soul to do it well. Unless you can commit everything you are to it, don't even start."

I still think about his words. I watch new clergy emerging in the church and I want to pull each of them aside and say, "Listen, this work will break your heart. It will make you jaded and twisted, if you're not careful, and sometimes even if you are. It will change you. The church is not rarefied; it's sanctified and it's made up of flawed people. You are one of them." My version of his blessing, I suppose.

Presence turned out to be key, after all.

It wasn't about how I presented myself, my physical appearance, or how I dressed. I still like to make a statement, though. I haven't found that presence during worship is key, either. Though that still point of worship, of gathering with others around a table in the swirling chaos of life, holds pure joy.

For me, ministry has always been about being present to the stories—the ones people are living, sharing, surviving, leaving, being born into.

"So…you went as far as you could in your last career," he said on that cold night when the ice wasn't just outside, but forming between us. And perhaps there was some truth in that.

As a journalist in another life long ago, I pursued the story, getting the details and answers to the five Ws, reporting it as best I could. Always the observer. Keeping the distance.

Now I see from inside the story. Often I cannot get the distance. Seldom do I find answers. There is only the story being lived out. And the Great Story Teller.

By the way, I found my parrot earrings this last move. I've started wearing them again.

About the Author

Bonnie Baird is an Anglican priest and writer, a mom and grandma, living and working along the South Shore of Nova Scotia.

Made in the USA
Charleston, SC
05 May 2016